A Cruising Guide to the Lower Seine

To Bill Mackie in commemoration
of the great birthday dinie hijack

D.
1991

A Cruising Guide to the Lower Seine

The River Seine to Paris including ports in the approaches

Written and compiled by E. L. Howells

Imray Laurie Norie and Wilson Ltd

St Ives Cambridgeshire England   1979

Published by **Imray Laurie Norie & Wilson Ltd**
St Ives Cambridgeshire England 1979

1st Edition ISBN 0 85288 068 5

This work incorporates the IALA System A buoyage which is to be introduced during 1979 and 1980.

Corrected to May 1979

Reproduced by C. L. Enterprises Ltd Fenstanton Cambridgeshire
Printed in Great Britain by Tabro Litho St Ives Cambridgeshire

Contents

Charts and Plans

Acknowledgements

The numerous French harbour masters and marina managers who readily answered my queries and provided valuable information.

My friend and partner Derek Bull who provided encouragement and advice at all times, filled gaps in my recollections and had the stamina to read and correct the written script.

My wife who took all the photographs, typed the manuscript, and acted as secretary and interpreter. Her skills and immunity to tedium made this book possible.

General

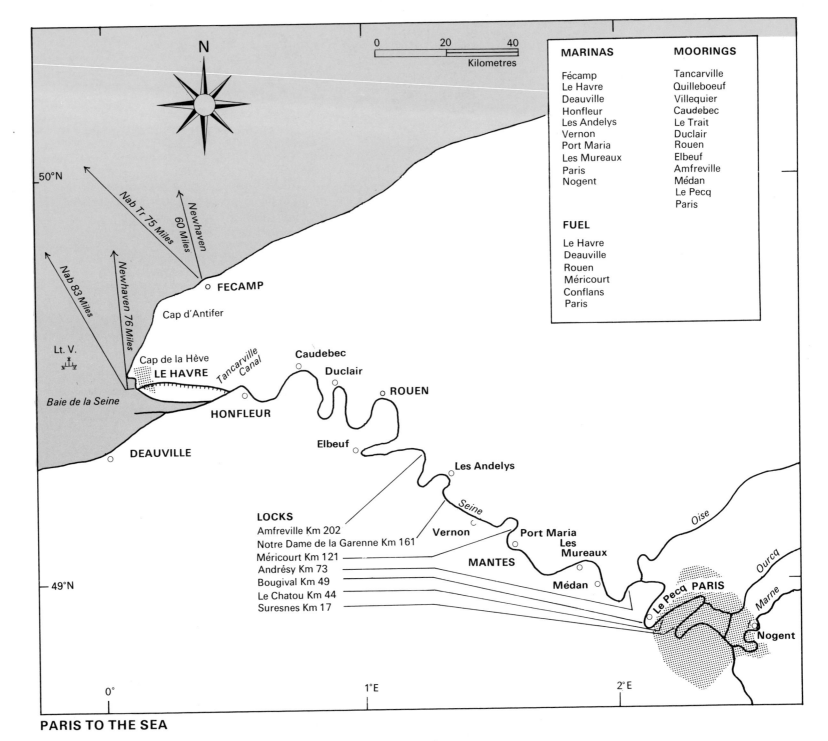

N

0　20　40
Kilometres

MARINAS

Fécamp
Le Havre
Deauville
Honfleur
Les Andelys
Vernon
Port Maria
Les Mureaux
Paris
Nogent

FUEL

Le Havre
Deauville
Rouen
Méricourt
Conflans
Paris

MOORINGS

Tancarville
Quilleboeuf
Villequier
Caudebec
Le Trait
Duclair
Rouen
Elbeuf
Amfreville
Médan
Le Pecq
Paris

50°N

Nab Tr 75 Miles
Newhaven 60 Miles
Nab 83 Miles
Newhaven 76 Miles

○ **FECAMP**

Cap d'Antifer

Lt. V.

Cap de la Hève
LE HAVRE
Tancarville Canal

Baie de la Seine

HONFLEUR

○ **DEAUVILLE**

Caudebec
Duclair ○
ROUEN

Elbeuf ○

Les Andelys
○

Seine

LOCKS
Amfreville Km 202
Notre Dame de la Garenne Km 161
Méricourt Km 121
Andrésy Km 73
Bougival Km 49
Le Chatou Km 44
Suresnes Km 17

Vernon
○

Port Maria
○ **Les**
Mureaux

MANTES

Médan ○

Oise

Ourcq

Le Pecq **PARIS**

Marne

Nogent

49°N

0°　　　1°E　　　2°E

PARIS TO THE SEA

1

Cruising in the Seine

The Seine is becoming increasingly popular with British yachtsmen, both as a gateway to central France and the Mediterranean and as a cruising ground in its own right. It is the most westerly point at which one can enter the inland waterway system of north-west Europe, the Brittany canals being isolated, and from here one can travel to Marseille, Hamburg or even Bucharest without ever seeing the sea. The Seine forms the first leg of the shortest route to the Mediterranean, a journey which takes at least a month.

Most people will settle for the trip to Paris which takes three or four days non-stop travelling although there is so much to see that a month could well be spent on the round trip.

The Seine is one of the longer rivers of France, 776 Km from its source in Burgundy to the sea at Le Havre. Its lower reaches from Paris to the sea are tortuous and winding and have given the river its name from Latin *sequana* – snake. Thus Paris is 200 Km from Le Havre in a straight line but 366 Km by river. The lower 164 Km from Amfreville, above Rouen, to the sea are tidal, although the once dreaded *mascaret* or bore now rarely occurs due to improvements in the estuary reach.

The mouth of the river has little of scenic note for the first few Km to Tancarville, as it flows through flat marshy country. Above Tancarville bridge the river becomes part of rural France at its most delightful; for here it commences a series of enormous meanders across a wide valley incised in a chalk plateau. The outside of each bend is overshadowed by chalk cliffs and wooded slopes whilst the inside is flat arable country. The only really large town is Rouen with its miles of dockland, the other towns being for the most part rather large villages. The last 50 Km into Paris is more built up, with a mixture of plush suburbia and industrial estates, until you round the last bend at Billancourt and the whole Paris skyline opens up before you.

This book does not dwell on the land-based attractions of Paris, regarded by many as the 'Queen of Cities'. The trip up the river through the heart of the city under its twenty-eight famous bridges and past the walls of Notre Dame is a fitting climax to the long journey.

Although whilst in the river the sea cannot have you and you can ignore gale and other warnings, there are certain hazards which may constrain your activities:

1. Fog is a frequent hazard in the mornings even in summer, occurring on about 10% of days between March and September. If it becomes really thick, one's only recourse is to anchor well out of the fairway and make the appropriate noises. (See page 6).

2. The tides in the river below Elbeuf run very strongly, up to 6 knots in places, and therefore determine the timing of your movements in the lower river. The regime of the tides is complex and will be explained fully on page 18 , but to summarize: by judiciously timing the departure soon after LW (or later for fast boats) flood tide can be carried to Rouen and beyond. Coming downstream a period of flood tide must be encountered and ebb cannot be carried all the way.

3. Ocean going ships, about twelve per day in each direction, ply up to Rouen and will generally ignore yachts in their path, as is their prerogative. Their movements are predictable, and they are therefore in themselves no danger, but the wash they cause can be uncomfortable, especially for boats at anchor. For this reason you should never secure to any fixed wharf or piles below Rouen. It is wiser to moor to a buoy or to anchor.

4. The once dreaded *mascaret* now occurs only between Quillebeuf and La Mailleraye and then only when the tide exceeds 8.5 m and the river is in flood.

5. The low bridges at Rouen prevent boats with masts higher than 6 m from proceeding further.

6. Above Amfreville there are frequent elongated islands (the equivalent of the *eyots* or *aits* of the Thames), the ends of which project as unmarked shoals up and downstream for up to 200 m.

7. Above Amfreville there is a great deal of driftwood, which cannot be readily seen and can damage propellers.

8. The current in the non-tidal river averages 1 knot (1.8 Kmph) in summer but can be much more in winter and spring.

9. There are seven locks in the non-tidal river, as well as one at each end of the Tancarville Canal. A French lock is not merely a slot in the ground such as you find on English narrow canals but resembles a miniature lake, maybe 220 m long and 17 m wide. The Tancarville locks are even bigger. As you will be sharing a lock with a 400 ton *péniche*, it is wise to evolve with your crew a prearranged drill for locking, as shouted improvisations cannot be heard above the rush of water and throb of engines. In the approach to a lock, give way to *péniches* close astern, as they are working, and you are on holiday. It is safer anyway to wait until they are tied up in the lock before entering.

Rouse out all your fenders and prepare two long warps, bow and stern, each double the rise of the lock. Inside the lock there are pegs in the walls to secure to but these are too far apart for small boats. When locking up, go alongside a ladder in the wall and send two of the crew up with the warps which can be taken around the bollards on the quay and back to the boat. Keep these taut at all times as there will be considerable turbulence when the water is let in. Do not cast off until the *péniches* have left as they take off on full power leaving a maelstrom behind. When locking down, pass the two warps around bollards and back to the boat, then slacken off as the level drops. If the rope jams, cast off the other end at once or the boat will be momentarily suspended before your cleats tear out. Locking is free, but at the quieter locks you may be expected to bandy French conversation with the *éclusier* and offer him an English cigarette. Locks are generally open from 0700 to 1930.

Buoyage

The French coast is usually far better marked than the English coast with much larger buoys. The area covered in this book is being converted to the IALA Buoyage System 'A' during 1979 but as the French have used a partly cardinal system for many years it is possible that some local anomalies may remain.

At the time of writing the following marks are in use:

Lateral Buoyage System *Used in well defined Channels*

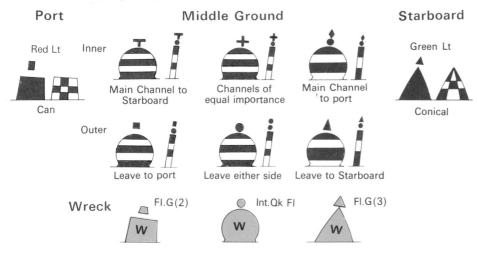

Cardinal Buoyage System

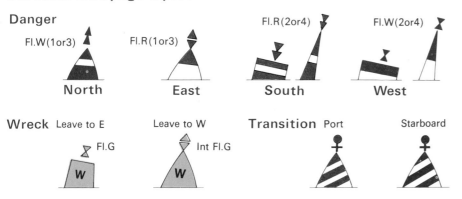

IALA Buoyage System A

LATERAL MARKS

Used generally to mark the sides of well defined navigable channels

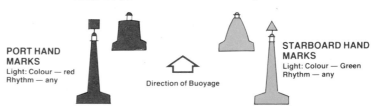

PORT HAND MARKS
Light: Colour — red
Rhythm — any

Direction of Buoyage

STARBOARD HAND MARKS
Light: Colour — Green
Rhythm — any

OTHER MARKS

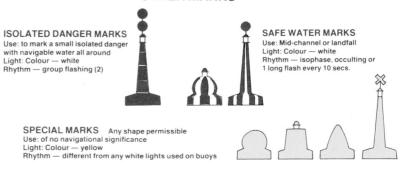

ISOLATED DANGER MARKS
Use: to mark a small isolated danger with navigable water all around
Light: Colour — white
Rhythm — group flashing (2)

SAFE WATER MARKS
Use: Mid-channel or landfall
Light: Colour — white
Rhythm — isophase, occulting or 1 long flash every 10 secs.

SPECIAL MARKS Any shape permissible
Use: of no navigational significance
Light: Colour — yellow
Rhythm — different from any white lights used on buoys

CARDINAL MARKS

Used to indicate the direction from the mark in which the best navigable water lies, or to draw attention to a bend, junction or fork in a channel, or to mark the end of a shoal.

LIGHTS: ALWAYS WHITE

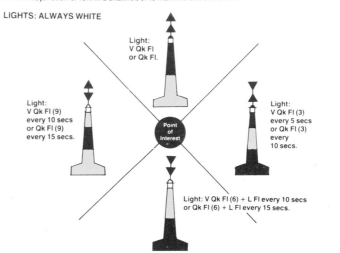

Light: V Qk Fl or Qk Fl.

Light: V Qk Fl (9) every 10 secs or Qk Fl (9) every 15 secs.

Point of Interest

Light: V Qk Fl (3) every 5 secs or Qk Fl (3) every 10 secs.

Light: V Qk Fl (6) + L Fl every 10 secs or Qk Fl (6) + L Fl every 15 secs.

Charts and Publications

The chartlets in this book are intended as a guide only and whilst sufficient for navigation in the river are no substitute for the appropriate charts of the coast. Furthermore a full account of all the land-based attractions of the Upper Normandy coast, the lower Seine valley and Paris itself is outside the scope of this book.

You will find the following publications useful:

Charts

C32 Baie de la Seine. Imray Laurie Norie & Wilson Ltd. Covers Fécamp, Deauville and beyond.
Carte Guide Navigation Côtière 1012. Available only in France, this chart is published by Editions Cartographiques Maritimes, 17 Rue Jacob, Paris. It covers the coast from Dieppe to Deauville and up the River to Rouen. Also published by Editions Maritimes are two atlases: *Paris à la Mer* and *Paris à Montereau*.

Other Publications

Guide Michelin – Normandie. A detailed guide on the geography, history and
   archaeology.
Guide Michelin – Paris.
Michelin Map 55. Le Havre to Paris 1:200,000.
AA Road Book of France. Gives useful street maps of French towns and a description of
   their history and sights to be seen.
Find Your Way in Paris. A street map and transport guide from the French Tourist
   Office, Piccadilly, London W.1.
Inland Waterways of France. E. E. Benest. This is the definitive guide to the canals and
   river of France. 4th edition published in 1978 by Imray Laurie Norie & Wilson Ltd.

Customs and Immigration

Arrival in France

You may enter France only at a permitted port of entry except when prevented by press of weather. Fécamp, Le Havre and Deauville are permitted ports, as for some reason is Rouen. It is no longer necessary for British yachts to fly a Q flag unless they have dutiable goods to declare. If you want a green card *(Passeport du Navire Etranger)* which may be required for passage through certain locks and will certainly be required to obtain duty free goods, apply at the customs house of the port of entry.

Immigration

A personal passport is required for each person on board, although in practice only the captain's is stamped.

Duty Free Stores

Spirits and tobacco can be bought up to certain limits at recognized stores on production of the green card and delivered to the boat. In theory you may only consume these at sea but in practice anywhere, as anyone who has seen the daily orgy at Cherbourg marina after the departure of the duty free truck will know. Duty free stores are available at Rouen (for boats going downriver), Le Havre and Deauville.

In France

You may keep your boat in France for more than six months out of twelve only if you go through the formalities of importing it and paying duty thereon.

Leaving France

In theory you should clear with Customs before leaving but nobody ever bothers. As far as English boats are concerned, French *douaniers* seem to regard their job as a well paid hobby, which is probably as it should be.

Fuel

Duty free fuel is no longer available for pleasure craft, and you will have to pay roadside pump prices for *gasoil* and for *essence*.

Equipment for Inland Waters

Even if your boat is seaworthy enough to cross the Channel certain additional equipment will be needed to venture without mishap or inconvenience into inland waters. Do not assume that because you are surrounded by land you are safer than at sea.

Power

Even if you intend to keep your mast up and turn back at Rouen, you are unlikely to be able to sail upriver. The tortuous course of the river, the hills and trees blanketing the wind, the proximity of shipping and the fierce tides make it not only difficult but dangerous unless one has local knowledge. You must therefore have an engine which will propel you at 5 knots for 10 hours if you wish to carry the flood tide to Rouen. (It is highly desirable that you should make the trip without stopping; see page 18). Many petrol engines, inboard and outboard, will not fulfill this requirement and you would be wise to test your engine beforehand if in doubt. It is difficult to obtain petrol in quantity between Le Havre and Rouen, so ensure that you have enough storage capacity for ten hours' running. Any spare petrol cans should be lashed on deck and not stored below.

Anchor

If you cannot make Rouen on one tide you may have to anchor in the tidal section, as mooring buoys are scarce, and you should not secure to any fixed structure below Rouen.

Depths in the river may be up to 12 m at HW, and the banks are steep-to, so that 40 m of cable is required. If you have to use rope to lengthen your cable, and this is not advisable, at least the lower third of the cable should be chain. Always buoy the anchor with stout rope, as the bottom is often foul.

Fenders

Above Rouen you will be rubbing shoulders, so to speak, with *péniches* in the locks or spending the night secured to a rough stone wall, so it is important to have plenty of fenders. Conventional fenders will not last long in the Seine, and old tyres are better. If you are concerned about smudges on your topsides, you can spend the preceding winter sewing the tyres into smart white canvas covers. Planks are useful to hang outside your fenders against piles or buttressed walls and occasionally to enable you to get ashore.

Horn

Sound signals are important in the river to give warning of your approach and intentions. A good stout hooter audible at 400 m is needed.

Crutch

If your mast is taller than 6 m, it must be lowered if you wish to pass the bridges at Rouen. This is best done at Le Havre or Deauville as there is no suitable place for the operation in the tidal section. Living with your mast on deck is trying,as it projects over the bow and stern and becomes an embarrassment at locks. A mast crutch in the cockpit will at least keep it out of your way and enable you to rig an awning when required. It is better to arrange mast storage at Le Havre or Deauville.

Flags

Red and blue flags 50 cm square are required by the traffic regulations.

Propeller

Because of the dangers of driftwood, a spare propeller is desirable if you can afford it. Places where a propeller can actually be changed are rare but it can take weeks to get one made if disaster does strike.

Spikes

In the non-tidal section, mooring to a quiet stretch of bank is possible in selected places, and you will need two mooring spikes to secure to. Even if you secure where there are bollards they are usually placed 40 m apart for the *péniches* so one spike will be needed. Warps should never be stretched across a towpath.

Bicycle

If you have room, a bicycle is useful for shopping in some of the riverside villages or even just for exploring the French countryside.

Traffic Regulations

Traffic Signs

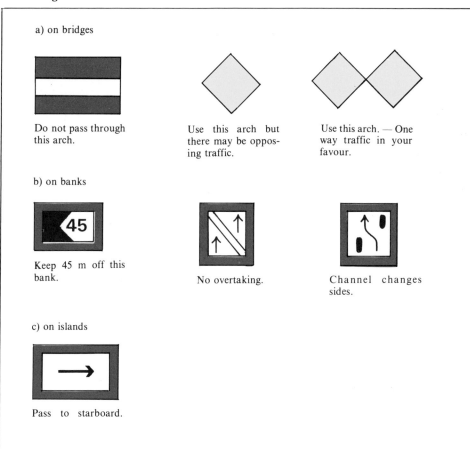

a) on bridges

Do not pass through this arch.

Use this arch but there may be opposing traffic.

Use this arch. — One way traffic in your favour.

b) on banks

45

Keep 45 m off this bank.

No overtaking.

Channel changes sides.

c) on islands

→

Pass to starboard.

The following regulations apply in the lower Seine between the sea and Paris:
1. Pleasure boats must not impede commercial navigation.
2. Do not moor or anchor in the navigable channel.
3. The speed limits are: tidal Seine — upstream 8 knots (15 Kmph)
                         tidal Seine — downstream 10 knots (18 Kmph)
                         non-tidal Seine — 6 knots (10 Kmph)
                         Canal de Tancarville — 5 knots (9 Kmph)

4. In fog you must stop when visibility is less than 300 m.
5. Keep to starboard except when otherwise indicated and overtake to port.
6. Give way to vessels travelling downstream or with the tidal current.
7. If you wish to keep to port when passing another vessel travelling in the opposite direction, fly a blue flag from the starboard side.
8. If you wish to turn, fly a red flag from that side.

Sound Signals

Long blasts are 4 seconds, short blasts are 1 second.

Attention.	—
I am going to starboard *or* I agree with your intention.	.
I am going to port *or* I disagree with your intention.	..
I am going astern.	...
I am unable to manoeuvre.	....
There is danger of collision *or* do not overtake.	.....
I am in distress.	— — —
I wish to overtake you to starboard.	— — .
I wish to overtake you to port.	— — ..
I am turning to starboard.	— .
I am turning to port.	— ..

In fog: one peal of bells — pass me to port.
In fog: two peals of bells — pass me to starboard.

Part I Ports of Entry

The constraints placed on your movements by the tides in the river mean that you will have to poise yourself in one of the ports at the mouth of the river to await the optimum time of departure upstream. In any case the crossing from England will take much of a day in most boats, so that an overnight stop is desirable.

Le Havre is the obvious candidate, being easy of access and well sheltered and giving the option of using the Canal de Tancarville as a last resort to bypass the estuary in rough weather.

Deauville has some tidal restrictions, and can become weatherbound, but there is much to beguile you into a few days of waiting.

Fécamp has been included as it is nearer to England (75 miles from the Nab Tower and only 60 miles from Newhaven) and the ebb tide can subsequently be used to bring along the coast to the estuary near the optimum time of starting up-river.

Honfleur cannot be used on the way up-river as it is open only around HW and you would then have an ebb tide in the river. It is possible to use it on the way down-river.

Ouistreham is unsuitable for your purposes as it is not open around LW and the ebbtide along the coast is adverse.

Fécamp: the twin piers from the S with a boat entering.

Fécamp

Fécamp, 75 miles from the Nab Tower and only 60 miles from Newhaven, is the nearest to England of the ports of entry. It is primarily a fishing port but a new marina built in 1975 has made it an ideal first stop for those who become bored on the longer Channel crossings. From Fécamp the ebb tide will carry you along the coast on the next stage of your journey to the river mouth in time to ascend the river to Rouen. If you become galebound, the town has its own excitements.

Restrictions on Entry
1. Strong winds between W and NE cause a steep sea off the entrance at low water.
2. The entrance is dredged to 1.5 m, but most yachts can enter at any time.
3. The Charpentier rocks, so called presumably because they cut up ships, lie to the NE of the entrance.

Tides
The streams offshore follow those in the English Channel generally, setting E from —0500 to HW Le Havre, then W, up to 2 knots at springs at 1 knot at neaps.
HW is HW Le Havre + 0027.
Duration of mean rise is 0540.
MHWS 8.0 m. MLWS 0.7 m. MHWN 6.4 m. MLWN 2.2 m.

Approach by Day
From afar the line of chalk cliffs about 100 m high appears unbroken, so that Fécamp, described by the pilot as lying in a cleft in the cliffs, is difficult to pick out. Furthermore, there are many minor clefts, so that false alarms and false optimism will abound. The features which distinguish Fécamp are the twin pierheads, the buildings of the town to the W and the white semaphore towers on the cliff to the E. Etretat, 8 miles to the W, lies in a similar cleft but has a church spire to the E, no pierheads and is smaller. In poor visibility the following features may be identified:
1. Cap d'Antifer lighthouse — a grey octagonal tower, 128 m high, 11 miles W of Fécamp.
2. The seawall of Port d'Antifer, 1 mile W of the Cap.
3. A line of port and starboard buoys labelled A9 to A26 extending 12 miles NW of the port.

In really poor visibility you can steer on a RDF bearing on Cap d'Antifer radio beacon (291.9 kHz. TI.) until you see the cliffs. If you cannot see the cliffs when you reach the 10 m depth contour you should stand off or anchor. A reed on Fécamp pier head sounds 2 blasts every 30 seconds from local HW —0300 to +0300.

Within a mile of the entrance beware the Charpentier rocks to the NE of the pierheads. Keeping the S pierhead open of the N pierhead will enable you to clear these.

Pass between the pierheads, and beyond the inner end of the S pier turn to starboard to enter the marina. Visitors normally secure to C pontoon, A being the nearest to the channel.

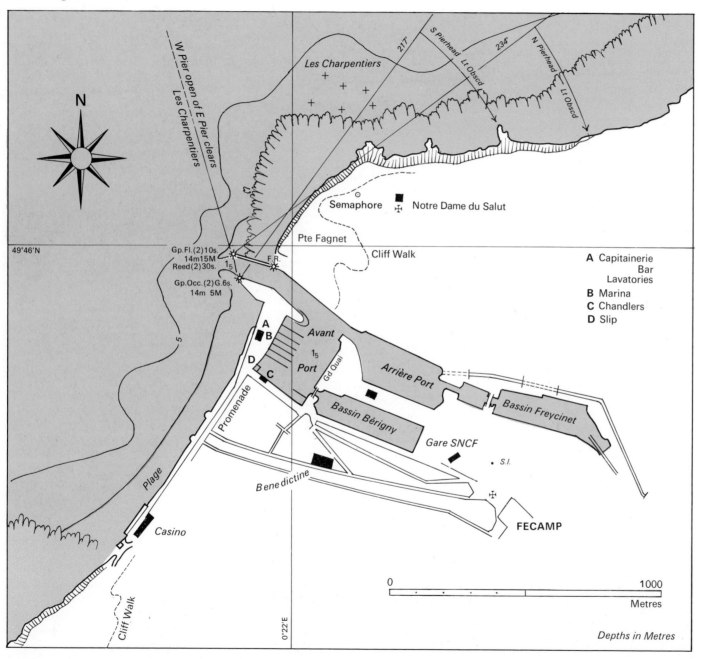

FECAMP –
APPROACH AND HARBOUR

Les Charpentiers

217° S Pierhead 234° N Pierhead
Lt Obscd   Lt Obscd

W Pier open of E Pier clears
Les Charpentiers

N

49°46'N

Semaphore Notre Dame du Salut

Pte Fagnet

Cliff Walk

Gp.Fl.(2)10s.
14m15M
Reed(2)30s.

F.R.

Gp.Occ.(2)G.6s.
14m 5M

A Capitainerie
    Bar
    Lavatories
B Marina
C Chandlers
D Slip

A
B

Avant

D

C

Port

Gd Quai

Arrière Port

Bassin Freycinet

Promenade

Bassin Bérigny

Gare SNCF

S.l.

Plage

Benedictine

FECAMP

Casino

Cliff Walk

0°22'E

0   1000
                              Metres

Depths in Metres

Approach by Night

The following lights will be seen:

Cap d'Antifer Fl. 20 sec. 128 m. 30M. Situated 11 miles SW of Fécamp.

Yport leading lights Occ. 4 sec. 11M in line lead 165° true.

Fécamp South pierhead Gp Occ (2). 6 sec. 14 m. 5M. Obscured by cliffs when bearing more than 217° true.

Fécamp North pierhead Gp Fl (2). 10 sec. 15 m. 16M. Obscured by cliffs when bearing more than 234° true.

Fécamp: the outer harbour from the N cliff. The entrance channel and the S pier in the foreground. The visitors' moorings right middle distance

Moorings and Facilities

The marina has been built by the delightfuly simple expedient of putting pontoons in part of a fishing harbour, although there have been concomitant improvements to the adjacent quay. It is a popular port of call for Dutch and Belgian and German yachts working their way down the coast. Water and free electricity are laid on, and there are lavatories and a bar in the *capitainerie* nearby. Charges are moderate, about 3 francs per metre per day, the second night being free, and include free miniature bottles of

Benedictine for as many crew members as you claim to have. There is a chandler on the quay, two large marine engineering establishments along the Bassin Bérigny and a 15 ton crane available through the *chef du port*.

For a longer stay you can lock into the Bassin Bérigny, open HW Le Havre —0100 to +0030, where charges are lower.

Fécamp: the outer harbour facing N. Visitors' moorings on the left. The inner end of the S pier can be seen with a sailing boat leaving. The semaphore tower is on the cliff

Fécamp: the outer harbour from seaward with visitors' moorings
The entrance to Bassin Bérigny in the background

Amenities

As Fécamp is a seaside resort as well as a fishing port, the restaurants are fairly expensive and tend to concentrate on fish and seafood of various types, but there is plenty of choice within these limitations. The beach is just over the wall from the marina, but this nearest part is suitable only for fakirs, being built from large pebbles with a precipitous slope down to the sea! If you stroll along the promenade to the W past the casino (a humbler establishment than that at Deauville) you will reach a more civilized sandy stretch.

In the town you can walk along the quay to the Bassins where the fishing boats unload or to the *distillerie* where for 2 francs you can endure a film on the manufacture of Benedictine for the sake of a few free snorts before lunch. On energetic days you can climb up to the cliffs on either side of the town and walk along the springy turf at the top as far as you wish. The small resorts of Yport and Etretat are within reach to the West. The cliff to the East give panoramic views of the harbour.

Pilotage — Fécamp to Le Havre

For this coastwise trip it is best to ensure a fair tide, which means leaving after HW Le Havre +0030 and arriving at Le Havre before LW. The total distance is 22 miles, and the tide averages $2^1/_2$ knots at springs and $1^1/_2$ knots at neaps. In reasonable visibility the navigation is straightforward. It is sufficient to keep within sight of the cliffs but outside the 10 m line most of the way. Just W of Cap d'Antifer the concrete jetty of Port d'Antifer projects 1 mile WNW, causing a minor tide race in westerly winds. Beware of tankers moving in the buoyed channel which extends 12 miles from the port. It is safe to approach within 1 mile of Cap de la Hève in 5 m, then steer SE to join the buoyed channel to Le Havre about $^1/_2$ mile out. This is a pleasant trip after the boredom of the Channel crossing, with views of the impressive chalk cliffs and glimpses of Yport and Etretat nestling in their narrow valleys.

Tides in the Seine Estuary

Well offshore, outside the Seine estuary, the tidal streams are a modification of those in the English Channel, setting SW from HW Le Havre +0400 to —0300; then NE from HW —0300 to +0400; the rates not exceeding 1.5 knots at springs. In the estuary the stream floods into the river from —0530 to +0030, reaching 3 knots at springs, then ebbs at up to 2.4 knots, running fair with the dredged channel in each case. The reclamation works projected for the area N of the Chenal de Rouen will presumably increase these rates.

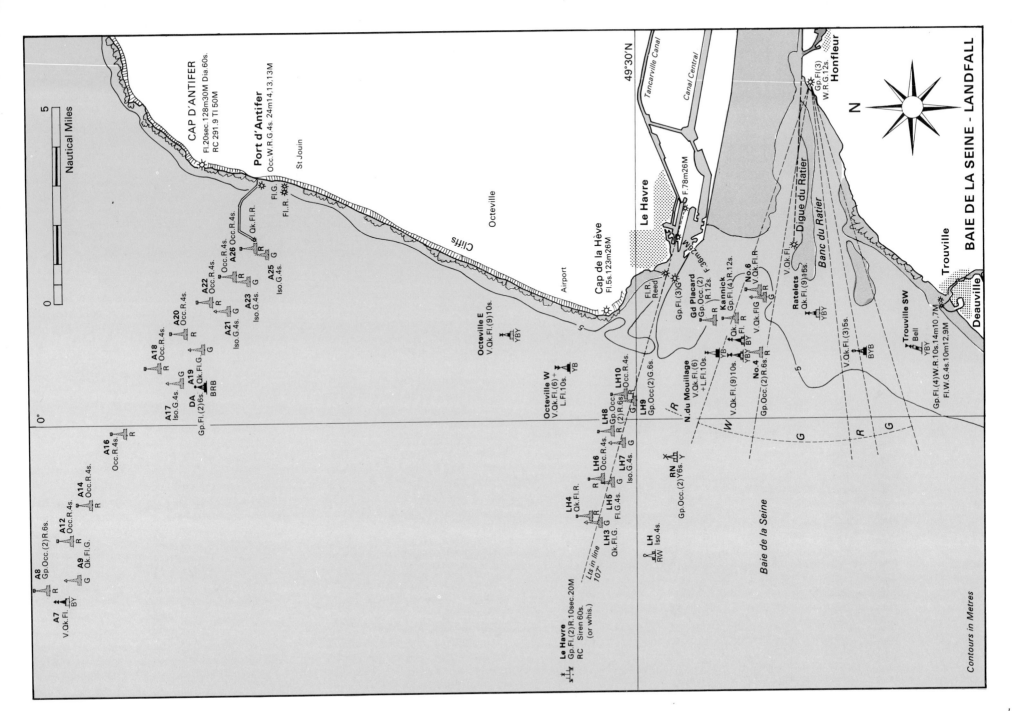

BAIE DE LA SEINE - LANDFALL

Nautical Miles

5

0

Contours in Metres

N

CAP D'ANTIFER
Fl.20sec.128m30M Dia.60s.
RC 291.9 Tl 50M

Port d'Antifer
Occ.W.R.G.4s. 24m14,13,13M

St Jouin

Octeville

Cliffs

Airport

Cap de la Hève
Fl.5s.123m26M

Octeville E
V.Qk.Fl.(9)10s.
YBY

Octeville W
V.Qk.Fl.(6)+
L.Fl.10s.
YB

Le Havre
F.78m26M

F. 36m26M

Fl.R.
Reed

Fl.R.

Le Havre
Gp.Fl.(2)R.10sec. 20M
RC   Siren 60s.
(or whis.)

49°30'N

0°

Tancarville Canal

Canal Central

Honfleur
Gp.Fl.(3)
W.R.G.12s.

Digue du Ratier

Banc du Ratier

Trouville

Deauville

V.Qk.Fl.

Ratelets
Qk.Fl.(3)15s.
YBY

V.Qk.Fl.(3)15s.
BYB

Trouville SW
Bell
YBY
Gp.Fl.(4)W.R.10s.14m10.7M
Fl.W.G.4s.10m12.9M

No.6
Gp.Fl.(4)R.12s. V.Qk.Fl.R
R

Kannick
Gp.Fl.(2) V.Qk.Fl.R.12s.
YB Qk. Fl.
Fl. R

No.4
V.Qk.Fl.(9)10s. Gp.Occ.(2)R.6s.
YB BY R

Gd Placard
V.Qk.Fl.(6)
+L.Fl.10s.

N.du Mouillage
Gp.Occ.(2)G.6s.
R

Gp.Fl.(3)G

R

W

G

R

G

G

R

A8
Gp.Occ.(2)R.6s.

A7
V.Qk.Fl.
BY

A9
G   Qk.Fl.G.

A12
R Occ.R.4s.

A14
R Occ.R.4s.

A16
R Occ.R.4s.

A17
Iso.G.4s. G

A18
R Occ.R.4s.

A20
R Occ.R.4s.

A19
G
DA
Gp.Fl.(2)6s. Qk.Fl.G.
BRB

A21
Iso.G.4s. G

A22
R Occ.R.4s.

A23
Iso.G.4s. G

A25
Iso.G.4s. G

A26 Occ.R.4s.
R   Qk.Fl.R.
G

Fl.G.

Fl.R.

LH
RW Iso.4s.

LH3
Qk.Fl.G.

LH4
Qk.Fl.R.

LH5
G Fl.G.4s.

LH6
R Occ.R.4s.

LH7
Iso.G.4s. G

LH8
Gp.Occ.
R (2) R.6s.
G

LH9
Gp.Occ.(2)G.6s.

LH10
Occ.R.4s.
R
G

RN
Gp.Occ.(2)Y6s. Y

Lts in line
107°

Baie de la Seine

Le Havre

Le Havre is the most convenient of the ports of entry but is probably the least interesting. Now the second largest port of France, it was extensively damaged during the war and has been rebuilt on the grand scale but in a soulless style. Anywhere in Le Havre is a considerable distance from everywhere else and one's abiding memory of the place will probably be of tramping along the endless wide concrete avenues in search of a restaurant or a post office. The new marina opened in 1974 has doubled the space available for visitors but has little else to recommend it being situated far from the town. The main advantages of Le Havre as a port are the easy well lit entrance and the link with the Tancarville Canal making you independent of weather for going upriver.

Restrictions on Entry

Strong winds from SW to NW cause a steep sea in the shallow water on each side of the approach channel, and this is often accentuated by waves reflected off the sea walls on either side of the entrance. Under these conditions it is best to stay in deep water for as long as possible by joining the approach channel well offshore.

Tides

Le Havre is a standard port.

HW is HW Dover —0103. MHWS 7.8 m. MHWN 6.4 m. MLWS 1.2 m. MLWN 2.6 m.

Duration of mean rise is 0540 and there is a stand of 2 hours at HW. Streams in the harbour are negligible but off the entrance set SE from —0500 to +0300 and then NW, never exceeding 1.5 knots.

Approach by Day

On the approach from England the first conspicuous feature is the continuous line of white cliffs 100 m high which extend from Cap de la Hève to the Somme estuary. The coast W of the Seine estuary is low-lying and will not be visible at this stage. The following landmarks may be seen:

Cap d'Antifer lighthouse, a grey octagonal tower 128 m high 10 miles N of Le Havre.

The prominent breakwater of Port d'Antifer just S of the Cap.

A double line of port and starboard buoys extending 12 miles NW from the breakwater.

Cap de la Hève lighthouse, a white tower with a red top 123 m high, just N of Le Havre.

In clear weather landfall should be easy as you merely identify the cliffs and follow them to their southern end when the buildings of Le Havre become visible.

Le Havre entrance is approached by a line of port and starboard buoys extending 6 miles WNW. In calm weather you need not join the buoyed channel until you are ¹/₂ mile out. In fact it is wise to stay out of it for as long as possible so as to leave room for big ships. In rough westerly winds the calmest weather will be found in the channel or just to the S of it, and under such conditions you should join the channel as far out as possible

to take advantage of this shelter. The entrance lies between the prominent breakwaters of the Digues Nord and Sud. The port entry signals on the enormous white semaphore tower inside the entrance are for big ships only.

In poor visibility the approach is more difficult but the cliffs may be approached to the 5 m contour. There are fog signals from:

Cap d'Antifer. Diaphone 60 seconds.

Le Havre lightvessel. Siren 60 seconds (may be replaced in summer by a whistle).

Digue Nord Head. Reed 15 seconds.

With RDF on 291.9 kHz you can fix on the following radio beacons, each transmitting every 6 minutes:

Cap d'Antifer. TI, range 50 miles.

Le Havre lightvessel. LH, range 30 miles.

Pointe de Ver. éR, range 20 miles.

Having used these aids steer for the channel buoys to Le Havre. When Le Havre lightvessel is off station in summer it is replaced by a buoy with a radio beacon on 296.5 kHz, call sign BG, range 10 miles, continuous.

Inside the entrance turn to port behind the Digue Nord then to starboard behind the marina mole and the new marina will be revealed to you. Visitors' moorings are on the near side of the nearest pontoon. Secure bow to the pontoon and stern to one of the row of white buoys, a tricky procedure in a W wind, especially as at HW some of the buoys submerge.

Approach by Night

The following lights will be seen from afar:

Cap d'Antifer Fl. 20 sec. 128 m. 30M.

Port d'Antifer Occ. WRG. 4 sec. 24 m. 14, 13, 13M. Green 068° - 078°, White 078° - 088°, Red 088° - 098°.

Cap de la Hève Fl. 5 sec. 123 m. 24M.

Le Havre lightvessel Gp Fl (2) R. 10 sec. 20M.

Fix your position by any of these lights that can be identified and steer for the deep channel buoys which are lit R or G. The street lights of Le Havre are unmistakeable but are obscured by Cap de la Hève when this bears more than 130° true. The entrance itself is lit by:

Digue Sud Head Gp Fl. (3) G. 2 sec. 15 m. 12M.

Digue Nord Head Fl R. 5 sec. 15 m. 24M.

Leading lights F. 36, 78 m. 26M, intensified 106° - 108°. Lead 107°.

In practice the entrance is so well lit that the leading lights can be ignored and it is enough to proceed between the reds and the greens until you pass between the *Digues*.

Moorings and Facilities

The marina has been doubled in size by the construction of the mole, the former marina N of the Digue Olsen now being largely reserved for the smaller club boats and the fishing fleet. The mole has not been built quite high enough, as at HW in strong westerly winds waves break over it so that the visitors' pontoon flexes and sways in an alarming

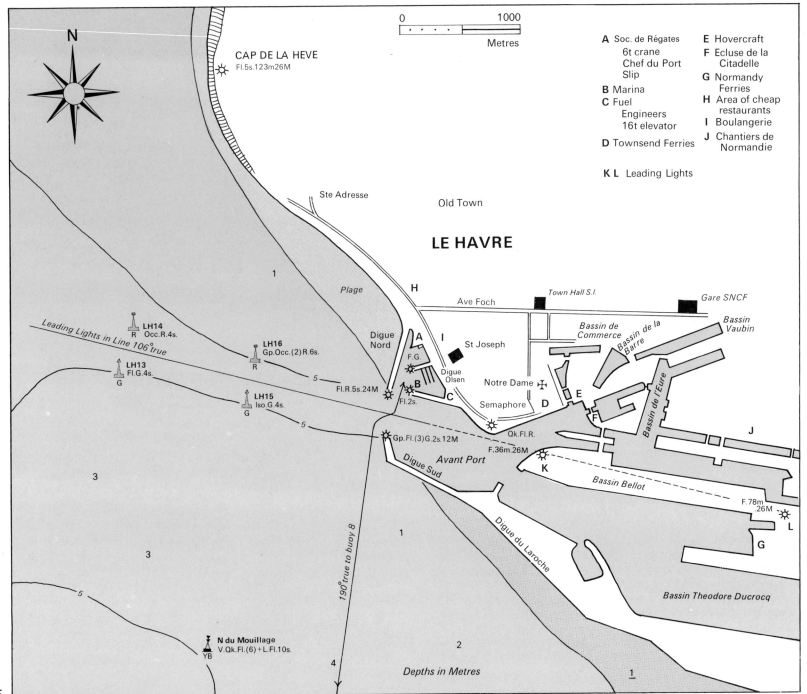

0   1000

Metres

A Soc. de Régates   **E** Hovercraft
    6t crane   **F** Ecluse de la
    Chef du Port   Citadelle
    Slip   **G** Normandy
B Marina   Ferries
C Fuel   **H** Area of cheap
    Engineers   restaurants
    16t elevator   **I** Boulangerie
D Townsend Ferries   **J** Chantiers de
                   Normandie

K L Leading Lights

CAP DE LA HEVE
Fl.5s.123m26M

N

Ste Adresse

Old Town

LE HAVRE

Plage

H

Ave Foch

Town Hall S.I.

Gare SNCF

Bassin Vaubin

Leading Lights in Line 106° true

LH14
R   Occ.R.4s.

LH16
Gp.Occ.(2)R.6s.
R

Digue Nord

A

I

St Joseph

Bassin de Commerce

Bassin de la Barre

LH13
Fl.G.4s.
G

B

Digue Olsen

Notre Dame

Bassin de l'Eure

LH15
Iso.G.4s.
G

F.G.

Fl.2s.

C

Semaphore

D

E

F

J

5

Fl.R.5s.24M

Qk.Fl.R.

5

Gp.Fl.(3)G.2s.12M

F.36m.26M

K

3

Avant Port

Bassin Bellot

F.78m
.26M

L

Digue Sud

190° true to buoy 8

3

1

Digue du Laroche

G

5

N du Mouillage
V.Qk.Fl.(6)+L.Fl.10s.
YB

Bassin Theodore Ducrocq

4

2

Depths in Metres

1

LE HAVRE

13

fashion. At LW life is quieter, but the exposed evil-smelling mud around the edges of the basin gives your mooring a certain ambience in hot weather. Facilities are disappointing; there is no electricity and water is laid only to a tap at the end of the pontoon. It is a long walk to the clubhouse of the Société des Régates du Havre, where you may use the showers, lavatory and bar after signing the visitors' book to mark the occasion. The marina office is just beyond the clubhouse. Mooring charges are expensive for what is supplied (3 francs per metre per day).

Fuel is available from the Tanguy Marine wharf at the SE corner of the basin where engine repairs of moderate complexity and chandlery are also obtainable. The 16 ton crane here is under the control of the marina. Near the clubhouse is a 6 ton crane and a precipitous slip where it is possible to dry out at LW. You may lower and store your mast by negotiation with the marina manager. For marine engineering of great complexity, apply to Chantiers de Normandie, a big ship concern who will work miracles on small boats at short notice but at a price. They are probably best for insurance jobs. Duty free stores can be obtained from the Société Normande Approvisionnement, 14, Rue Après Mannevillette, Tel. 22-66-75. (Take Rue Jules Lecesne running E from the Place de l'Hotel de Ville, turn left on Rue Après Mannevillette after 200 m.)

Amenities

Le Havre is now an enormous sprawling city based on the port and the industrial complex to the east. The main streets built after the war are laid out on a scale which dwarfs the mere pedestrian. The Avenue Foch is typical: leading from the seafront near the marina to the centre, it is fully 200 m wide, lined with trees and flanked by a monotonous perspective of concrete flats tapering into the distance. At the centre, the Hotel de Ville is built twenty storeys high to overawe the rate-payers and other attractions include the cathedral which resembles a Saturn V rocket on a launch pad with buttressed fins and tiny portholes. There are some pleasant areas, however; near the town centre is the Bassin de Commerce, once the main dock basin and now a boating lake, spanned by a whimsical but otiose pedestrian suspension bridge. Until recently the Bassin was used for yacht moorings but on Christmas Eve 1975 the lock gates collapsed, and the water rushed out leaving many boats hanging on their warps before they crashed to the bottom. The damage is still the subject of litigation and the nearby quays are littered with wrecks presumably waiting to be used in evidence. The old town, untouched by war or the architects, lies to the north and has narrow winding streets which reveal occasional glimpses of the sea.

The sandy beach is just north of the marina past a region of beach huts and candy floss stalls and even in the season it is possible to find a quiet spot if you walk far enough. If it's too cold to swim you can continue beyond the beach to Ste Adresse then up the cliff to Cap de la Hève lighthouse whence there is a panoramic view of the coast to Fécamp, the Seine estuary and the port of Le Havre.

The best restaurants are just along the front by the marina office and the all-important *boulangerie* is in the street north of the *cathédrale*.

In summer there are four or five boats a day to Portsmouth or Southampton making changing of crews easy.

Deauville

Deauville, 88 miles from the Nab Tower, is the furthermost from England of the three ports of entry. It is, however, probably the most interesting. The town itself displays an opulence no longer seen in Britain and hotel prices are such that the only way to stay there is on a boat. The new marina, opened in 1975, enables one to enter at most stages of the tide and moor in peace and relative seclusion yet with the famous beach within a few minutes' walk. The marina charges are expensive by French standards, but the old wet basins, cheaper but less accessible, are still available.

Restrictions on Entry

1. Strong winds from NW to N cause a steep sea in the shallow water offshore and Le Havre is safer under these conditions.
2. The entrance channel (in 1978) dries 1.5 m between the training walls confining entry in a boat of 1 m draft to HW —0340 to +0540 at springs, HW —0440 to +0640 at neaps.
3. Above the marina entrance the river channel dries 2.5 m restricting entry with 1 m draft to HW —0300 to +0400.
4. The lock gates into the wet basin open in free flow from HW —0300 to +0230 but you can anchor immediately outside in mud drying 1.8 m.
5. The marina lock does not open between 2300 and 0700 in winter but you can anchor in the pool outside in 2.5 m.

Tides

HW Deauville is HW Dover —0138 or HW Le Havre —0035.
MHWS 7.7 m. MHWN 6.4 m. MLWS 1.0 m. MLWN 2.4 m.
Duration of mean rise is 0510 and there is a stand of 2 hours after HW.
Streams in the offing are weak, not exceeding 1.4 knots at springs, setting E on the flood and W on the ebb.

Approach by Day

In good visibility from afar the buildings of the town are obvious and lie about 3 miles E of the prominent Mont Canisy ridge. From Trouville SW bell buoy with a W cardinal topmark) the entrance bears 116° true 1.3 miles. Make for a position 1 mile from the entrance at the outer end of the dredged channel with the leading marks in line 150° true: front — a white tower with a red top 11 m high at the outer end of the E jetty; rear — a similar tower 17 m high at the root of the E jetty.

To confuse you, a third tower, again white with a red top 14 m high, lies in front of and in line with those at the end of the 500 m long submerged E training wall.

The dredged channel must be followed especially at low water as the sands on each side dry up to 3 m. The outer end of the 550 m W training wall is marked by a white framework tower with a green top 10 m high. Both training walls dry up to 4 m, being

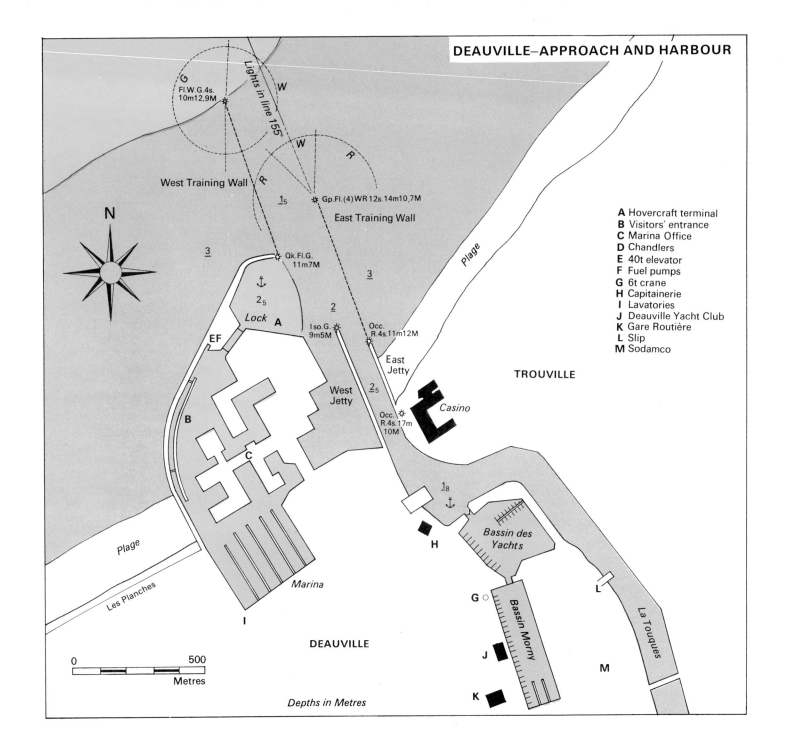

DEAUVILLE–APPROACH AND HARBOUR

G Fl.W.G.4s. 10m12,9M

Lights in line 155°

W

W

R

R

West Training Wall

1₅

Gp.Fl.(4)WR 12s.14m10,7M

East Training Wall

N

3

Qk.Fl.G. 11m7M

3

2₅

Plage

A Hovercraft terminal
B Visitors' entrance
C Marina Office
D Chandlers
E 40t elevator
F Fuel pumps
G 6t crane
H Capitainerie
I Lavatories
J Deauville Yacht Club
K Gare Routière
L Slip
M Sodamco

Lock   A

EF

Iso.G. 9m5M

2

Occ. R.4s.11m12M

B

West Jetty

East Jetty

C

2₅

Occ. R.4s.17m 10M

Casino

TROUVILLE

1₈

Bassin des Yachts

H

Plage

Les Planches

G

L

Bassin Morny

I

Marina

DEAUVILLE

J

La Touques

K

M

0   500
Metres

Depths in Metres

marked by poles with the appropriate topmarks, and must not be crossed.

After passing the front leading mark you will see the marina entrance to starboard behind an enormous seawall. Follow the small starboard buoys to the lock which is in free flow when the tide is above 5.5 m but otherwise opens fairly promptly. In the lock secure to the ingenious bollards which float up and down in grooves chased in the walls. Inside the marina, secure to the long curving visitors' pontoon to starboard; the residential moorings are further on beyond the flats.

For the old wet basins eschew the starboard turn into the marina and continue up the main channel between the jetties, favouring the starboard side which is deeper. Depths vary from drying 1.5 m opposite the marina entrance to drying 2.5 m abeam of the rear leading mark then 1.8 m outside the basin gates. The gates open in free flow from HW —0030 to +0230 but you can wait at anchor in the pool outside the marina lock in 2.5 m or dry out opposite the slipway outside the gates in mud and shingle drying 1.8 m. In the latter spot the ebb runs hard towards low water so it is wise to be well anchored. When the gates open enter the basin and secure to the visitors' pontoons or to the quays anywhere except on the W side, mooring to the quay being by the stern with the bow to a buoy. Allow for up to 2 m rise when the gates are open.

The river Touques, reached by turning to port before the gates, dries high and there are no visitors' moorings. It is here that the enormous fishing fleet rests.

By Night

Trouville SW buoy is unlit but the lights of the town are visible from afar. Make for a position one mile from the entrance with the leading lights in line 150° true. These are:

Front: Occ. R. 4 sec. 11 m. 12M intensified 060° - 150°.

Rear: Occ. R. 4 sec. 17 m. 10M synchronized with the front visible 120° - 170°.

The **outer end of the E training wall** in line with these leading lights is marked by a light Gp Fl (4). WR. 12 sec. 14 m. 10,7 M showing red from the shore to 131°, white 131° - 175°, red 175° to the shore.

On the starboard side of the channel, the lights are as follows:

Outer end of W training wall: Fl. WG. 4 sec. 10 m. 12,9M. White 005° - 176°, green 176° - 005°.

End of marina seawall Qk Fl.G 11 m. 7M.

End of W. Jetty Iso G. 4 sec. 9 m. 5M.

Red and green lights are shown at the marina lock to control entry.

Moorings and Facilities

The new marina called Port Deauville to distinguish it from the older basins, the Port de Deauville, is the biggest on the channel coast of France with 950 berths, 60 of which are for visitors. It was built on the grand scale by excavating part of the seafront gardens and constructing a 750 m seawall out from the main beach to enclose 12 hectares of water. On the landward side a complex of futuristic flats, shops and a hotel has been built; whilst arms of water with private pontoons extend between the flats. Charges are high by French standards (about 5 francs per metre length per day in summer, the second night being free) but there is good value for money. Water and free electricity are laid to each

Deauville: the marina. Visitors' pontoon to right

berth, and the charge includes a 3 franc voucher for each of the crew to shower in the subterranean ablutions, which, incidentally, open shop hours only. There are chandlers in the shopping centre and a 40 ton elevator in the marina. Fuel is available except when the lock is in free flow as the pumps are cunningly situated on the other side of the lock from the lock keeper who has the key.

Only the outer of the two old basins, Bassin des Yachts, is available for visitors, the inner, Bassin Morny or Gare Routière, being reserved for commercial boats. Report to the *capitainerie* at the W corner of the outer basin. Charges are more moderate than in the new marina, about 3 francs per metre per day in summer, the second day being free. At the Deauville Yacht Club nearby visitors are welcome to use the lavatories, bar and showers in whichever order they wish. This is incidentally about the only place in Deauville with a working telephone. There is a 6 ton crane under the control of the club who are also prepared to store your mast if you don't want to live with it during the voyage up the Seine. Duty free stores can be ordered from the strangely named Sodamco timber yard opposite the club. There is a boatyard and a marine engineers nearby. The customs house is at the head of the Bassin Morny.

Amenities

The town is well worth a day or two's stay between the rigours of a Channel crossing and the ascent of the Seine. The beach, two miles of golden sand, is just over the seawall from the marina. It is combed and brushed every morning by an army of council workmen to remove footprints and make it smooth to lie on. Behind the beach are Les Planches, a plank walk where once strolled the fashionable of Europe with their parasols but where now the rich matrons of Paris lie topless in the sun. Avert your gaze as you pass! There are many restaurants with fabulous menus at fabulous prices but the best buy is take-away food from the *charcuteries: pâtés,* sausages, salads and the like. You can go to the races just behind the town or even put on a tie and go to the casino (where there is 2 franc entry to exclude riffraff). On a cool day, when only the French will swim, you can walk for miles along the beach to Dives-Cabourg, the next port to the west.

Across the river is Trouville, which is less fashionable and slightly less expensive. Here there is another casino and another beach backed by a maze of narrow streets with restaurants for all tastes and pockets. Along the quayside there is a daily fishmarket where one can buy directly from the fishing boats. From Trouville it is possible to walk along the beach for 5 miles to Honfleur to reconnoitre the next move.

From just outside the marina lock a hovercraft runs hourly to near Le Havre ferry port making changing a crew easy. There are regular buses from the Gare Routière in each direction along the coast and trains to Caen and Paris.

Deauville: the residents' moorings and waterside flats.

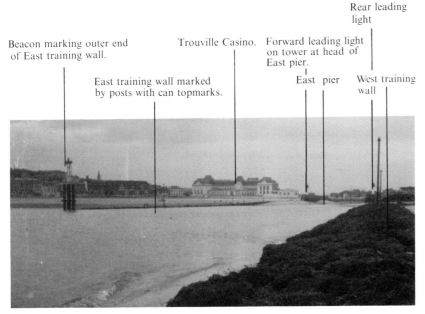

Beacon marking outer end of East training wall.

East training wall marked by posts with can topmarks.

Trouville Casino.

Forward leading light on tower at head of East pier.

Rear leading light

East pier

West training wall

Deauville: The entrance from the West training wall. Height of tide 2.5m

Part II The Sea to Rouen

Rouen, although only 53 miles (85 Km) in a straight line from the sea, is 78 miles (123 Km) by the meandering river. By timing the departure from the river mouth, however, even a 4 knot boat can complete the trip in 10 or 11 hours, carrying a flood tide all the way. The estuary is shallow so that in strong winds between WSW and NW the passage from Deauville or Le Havre to the river mouth can be exceedingly rough. Furthermore, due to the speed of the tide even in calm weather standing waves form in the Chenal de Rouen. As a last resort the Canal de Tancarville can be used to bypass the sea reach but this 'short cut' requires careful timing and may take up to 6 hours.

The first 25 Km of the river is flanked by training walls, beyond which marshy ground stretches to the hills in the distance. In the eighteenth century the river covered the full width of this valley but the need to provide a stable deep channel for navigation and to control the *mascaret* led to the building of training walls, the most recent of which was built in 1960. Further reclamation is planned for the mudbanks SE of Le Havre to enable the port and industrial complex to be extended.

Tancarville: the N end of the bridge. The lock entrance for small boats is at the foot of the bridge pier.

Above Tancarville the river begins a series of wide meanders, tacking from one side of the valley to the other, going about just in time under a chalk cliff or a steep forested hill and heading off through flat arable land until the next hill looms up. Through all this glide the ships from the ocean, looking incongruous against the green background, their wash curling up the sloping stone banks as they pass. There are many villages en route which are worth exploring but because of the wash from passing ships it is dangerous to secure alongside and uncomfortable to moor or anchor. Indeed the current is so strong and the depths so great that even anchoring is difficult, but there are mooring buoys at some villages. It is far better to enjoy the scenery as it goes by and wait until Rouen before setting foot on land.

After 120 Km the dockland appearing on the starboard hand gives warning of the approach of Rouen, the head of navigation for ocean going ships and yachts with masts.

Depths in the river are charted 4 m, giving up to 12 m at HWS. The range of tide decreases upriver but is still 2.9 m at Rouen and must be allowed for when anchoring.

Up to Tancarville the Chenal de Rouen is marked by port and starboard buoys lit at night by red and green lights. Above Tancarville there are miniature lighthouses on the banks lit at night mainly by fixed red and green or occasional violet lights. On the inside of each hairpin bend is often a lobe of shallows usually marked by a buoy apparently in midstream.

Tides in the River

The tidal regime in the river is at first sight exceedingly complex but after a certain amount of study becomes relatively simple to understand.

Table A — Tides related to HW Le Havre.

Place		Flood begins	Ebb begins	HW	Height (metres)	LW	Height (metres)
Estuary	Sp	−0500	+0030	−0540	7.8	0000	1.2
	Np				6.5		2.8
Tancarville	Sp	−0205	+0205	−0610	8.2	−0030	2.4
	Np	−0240	+0110		6.9		3.7
Caudebec	Sp	−0045	+0300	−0320	8.1	+0045	4.2
	Np	−0145	+0200		6.7		4.3
Duclair	Sp	+0115	+0400	−0045	7.8	+0320	4.7
	Np	−0015	+0425		6.6		4.9
Rouen	Sp	+0125	+0550	+0435	7.8	+0035	4.9
	Np	+0115	+0540		6.8		5.5

TIDAL STREAMS—ESTUARY TO ROUEN

Neaps -----
Springs ———

The times of slack water become progressively later upriver so that a boat leaving the estuary soon after LW can carry a fair tide all the way to Rouen. Below a 5 knot boat leaving in the hour after LW springs can arrive at Rouen in the last hour of the flood.

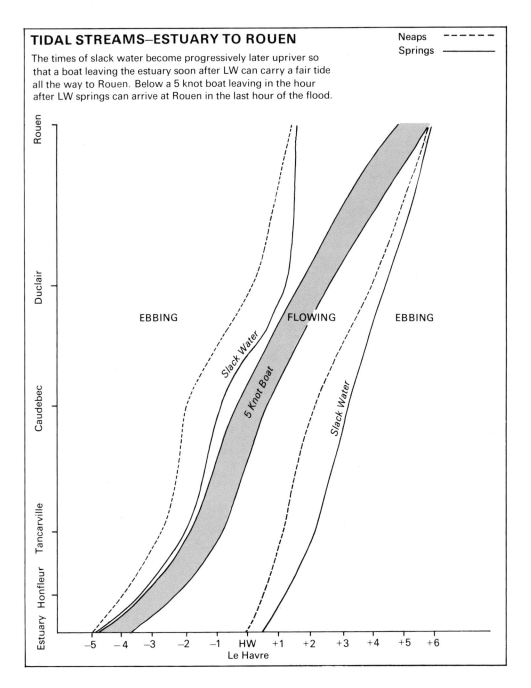

TIDAL STREAMS—ROUEN TO ESTUARY

As you proceed downriver on the ebb, slack water advances to meet you. Eventually you will have a foul tide and can anchor to await the next ebb or carry on downriver to meet it. Below a 6 knot boat gains an hour (but burns 3½ hour's extra fuel) by carrying on instead of anchoring.

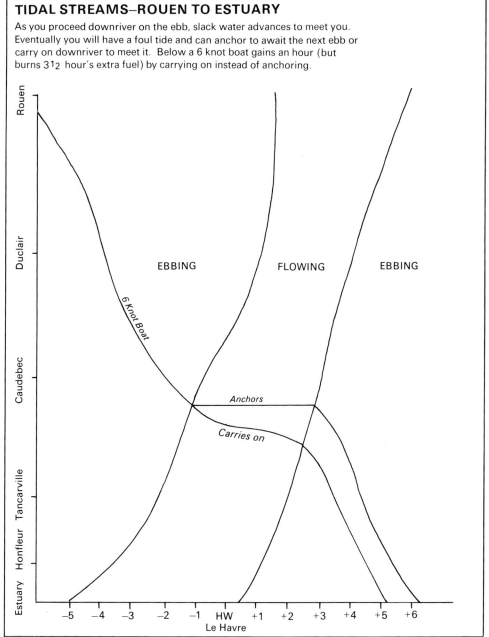

In the Baie de Seine the tide rises for about 5 hours from LW to HW, stands for 2-3 hours after HW then falls for 5 hours. This vertical oscillation of the sea sends twice daily 'waves' of HW up the river, so that the times of HW and LW travel upstream at about 14 knots. The wave as it travels becomes distorted, so that at any given point in the river the level rises for $1\frac{1}{2}$ - $4\frac{1}{2}$ hours, stands for $2\frac{1}{2}$ hours then falls for $5\frac{1}{2}$ - $8\frac{1}{2}$ hours. In the days of the *mascaret* the front of the wave was vertical and the level would rise 2- 3 m in the instant after LW. Nowadays the friction of the banks and bottom reduces the height of the wave, the spring range decreasing from 6.6 m at Le Havre to 2.9 m at Rouen.

Similarly the time at which the stream turns becomes later as you pass upriver. At any given point below Rouen the tide floods for $3\frac{1}{2}$ - $4\frac{1}{2}$ hours and ebbs for 8 - 9 hours, but a boat can follow the flood upriver.

All times are subject to modification by meteorological conditions and the amount of land water in the river. Spring rates are 6 knots on the flood and 4 knots ebb between Tancarville and Caudebec and about 3 knots above there, neap rates being $\frac{2}{3}$ of these values.

Table B — Optimum times for proceeding upriver on HW Le Havre

Speed of boat		Leave estuary	Arrive Rouen
5 knots	Sp	—0500 to —0400	+0445 to +0545
	Np	—0500	+0545
6 knots	Sp	—0500 to $\begin{matrix}-0255\end{matrix}$	$\begin{matrix}+0340\end{matrix}$ to +0545
	Np	—0400	+0445
7 knots	Sp	—0500 to $\begin{matrix}-0205\end{matrix}$	$\begin{matrix}+0250\end{matrix}$ to +0545
	Np	—0255	+0340
8 knots	Sp	—0500 to $\begin{matrix}-0120\end{matrix}$	$\begin{matrix}+0205\end{matrix}$ to +0545
	Np	—0205	+0250

If you start from the river mouth at or shortly after the start of the flood, you can carry a fair tide all the way to Rouen. If you start too late or your boat is too slow or you idle on the way you will be overtaken by the ebb tide and will have to anchor in the river. Table B shows the optimum times of leaving the estuary for boats of various speeds.

Although the ebb runs for 8 - 9 hours at any given point, coming downriver is more difficult; as you descend on the ebb a wave of flood tide is coming to meet you. If your boat is slow you may as well anchor to save fuel as the tide will begin to ebb in $3\frac{1}{2}$ - $4\frac{1}{2}$ hours. In a fast boat it is worth battling on against the flood as the further downriver you go the sooner the ebb starts. Table C guides your strategy going downriver.

Until the nineteenth century the river was wide and shallow below Tancarville, and the flood tide, when forced into the narrow reach above Tancarville, rose to form a vertical step in the water level which rushed upstream at 12 knots. This *mascaret* or bore was a hazard to all ships. The building of training walls in the estuary has tamed the river, and the *mascaret* now only occurs on days when HW Le Havre exceeds 8.5 m and the river is in flood and then only between Quilleboeuf and La Mailleraye. On these days soon after

local LW a steplike wave up to 2 m high runs upriver at 12 knots. If you are unlucky enough to be caught by the *mascaret* batten down all hatches, secure all loose gear and motor slowly into it, meeting it if possible on the inside of a bend, where the wave is smaller. If your boat is fast you can try to outrun it until it disappears at La Mailleraye.

Table C — Optimum times for proceeding downriver on HW Le Havre

Speed of boat		Leave Rouen	Arrive estuary	
5 knots	Sp	—0635 to —0515	$\begin{matrix}+0600\end{matrix}$ to +0725	Driving continuously
	Np	—0645 to —0540	+0620	
6 knots	Sp	—0635 to —0435	$\begin{matrix}+0525\end{matrix}$ to +0725	
	Np	—0645 to —0500	+0540	
7 knots	Sp	—0635 to —0225	$\begin{matrix}+0315\end{matrix}$ to +0725	
	Np	—0645 to —0205	+0325	
8 knots	Sp	—0635 to —0130	$\begin{matrix}+0220\end{matrix}$ to +0725	
	Np	—0645 to —0135	+0215	
5 knots	Sp	—0635	+0725	Anchoring on Flood
	Np	—0645	+0940	
6 knots	Sp	—0635 to —0535	$\begin{matrix}+0625\end{matrix}$ to +0725	
	Np		+0715	
7 knots	Sp	—0635 to —0435	$\begin{matrix}+0525\end{matrix}$ to +0725	
	Np	—0645 to —0535	+0615	
8 knots	Sp	—0635 to —0340	$\begin{matrix}+0430\end{matrix}$ to +0725	
	Np	—0645 to —0435	+0515	

Chenal de Rouen

The Chenal de Rouen is the dredged channel from the river mouth to off Honfleur. It is kept open at great expense by constant removal of the mud brought down by the river. Some years ago a training wall, the Digue du Ratier, was built to divert the river from its former course along the coast from Honfleur to off Trouville, and the deep channel now runs close parallel to this. The north side of the channel is bounded by shifting mudbanks which are shallower than charted and may dry in places. It is proposed to reclaim this area to expand the port of Le Havre.

The tidal streams run strongly in this channel (up to 4.5 knots at springs) and with westerly winds over the ebb an unpleasant sea with standing waves is set up. The approaches to the river mouth from both Le Havre and Deauville can be rough in onshore winds because of the shallow water and on the Le Havre side this is made worse by reflected waves off the Digue Sud.

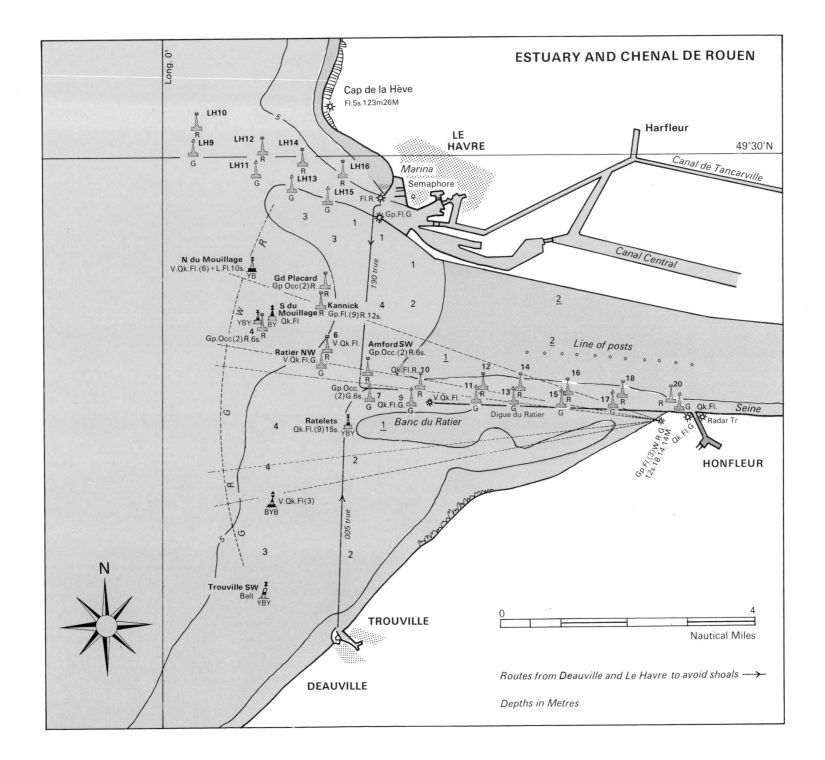

ESTUARY AND CHENAL DE ROUEN

Long. 0°

Cap de la Hève
Fl.5s.123m26M

LH10

LH9 R

LH12

LH14

LH11 G

LH16

LH13

LH15 R

Fl.R.

G

G

3

3

1

1

190 true

1

LE HAVRE

Harfleur

49°30'N

Canal de Tancarville

Marina
Semaphore

Gp.Fl.G

N du Mouillage
V.Qk.Fl.(6)+L.Fl.10s. YB

Gd Placard
Gp Occ(2)R. R

S du
Mouillage
YBY BY Qk.Fl

Kannick R
Gp.Fl.(9)R.12s.

Gp.Occ(2)R.6s. R
4

Ratier NW
V.Qk.Fl.G. R

6
V.Qk.Fl.
G

Amford SW
Gp.Occ.(2)R.6s.

Qk.Fl.R. 10

4

2

1

2

Line of posts 2

Gp.Occ.
(2)G.6s. 7
Qk.Fl.G. G

9
V.Qk.Fl.

12

14

16

18

20

11
R

13
R

15
R

17
R

R

R

G Qk.Fl. Seine

Ratelets
Qk.Fl.(9)15s. YBY

Banc du Ratier

Digue du Ratier

Radar Tr

Gp.Fl.(3)W.R.G.
12s.18.14.14M
Qk.Fl.G

HONFLEUR

4

4

1

2

V.Qk.Fl(3)
BYB

005 true

3

2

N

Trouville SW
Bell YBY

TROUVILLE

0   4

Nautical Miles

Routes from Deauville and Le Havre to avoid shoals →

DEAUVILLE

Depths in Metres

Approach

From Le Havre entrance make good a course of 190° true to reach the Chenal de Rouen at buoys Nos. 7 and 8. Any course to the east of this may pass over the drying mudbanks.

From Deauville make good 005° true to leave Les Ratelets buoy (black and white with a white topmark) close to starboard to avoid Les Ratelets bank, which dries 1 m, then steer for buoys Nos. 7 and 8.

In rough westerly weather it is better to join the main channel further west to stay in deep water as long as possible.

River

From here the Chenal de Rouen although narrow is well marked with port and starboard buoys for the next 16 miles to near Tancarville. On the starboard side is the Digue du Ratier, a training wall drying about 3-4 m, whose seaward end is marked by a large beacon. Behind the wall an area of drying sandbanks stretches to the low wooded hills west of Honfleur and represents the former course of the channel. To port is a line of posts with port topmarks which should be ignored as they lie well within shoal water. They probably represent the south edge of the proposed reclamation area.

Once you are in the river the flood tide running at 4 knots takes charge and you will be swept up at an encouraging rate. Soon to starboard Honfleur lighthouse appears and now well inland it marks the edge of the former river channel. The Digue becomes a continuous high masonry wall about half a mile below the entrance to Honfleur, which is marked by a white control tower. Whilst flashing past the entrance, perhaps at 10 knots, you catch a glimpse of Honfleur town. Above Honfleur the buoys become fewer but beware the port buoy apparently in midstream half a mile below Tancarville. The river continues past flat marshy country to starboard and drying mudbanks to port, although the hills can be seen in the distance, and ahead Tancarville bridge begins to dominate the scene.

Tancarville bridge, a single span of 640 m with 48 m headroom, was built in 1959 and is the lowest bridge on the river. Just below the bridge to port are the two locks to the Tancarville canal. It is possible to moor on the port side just above the bridge but the tide may reach 6 knots, which may make a visit to the attractive restaurant under the bridge an anxious procedure. From here on the distance to Paris is marked in Km (and for some reason $\frac{1}{40}$ Km) along the banks.

Honfleur: the painters at work in the inner basin.

Honfleur

Honfleur is a delightful spot to spend a day or so but cannot conveniently be used as a starting point for the trip upriver. It is open only for 2 hours around local HW so that one would have to wait in the approach channel until the next LW for a fair tide. Nor is it a permitted port of entry into France so that you must clear customs elsewhere. The best plan is to time the journey downriver to arrive at Honfleur soon before HW. The town was once a busy port but embankment of the Seine and progressive silting has now left it a quarter of a mile inland and attainable from the main river only by a narrow approach channel. Today it remains a tourist attraction because of its enclosed harbour, now a marina, and historic buildings.

Honfleur: the residents' pontoon

Restrictions on Entry

1. The approach channel has silted and now dries about 0.5 m in the middle and 3-4 m near the sides. A boat of 1 m draft might therefore ground at MLWS.

2. The Avant Port dries 3-4 m soft mud, confining entry to HW Le Havre —0200 to +0400.

3. The gates into the marina basin open for 2 hours from HW Le Havre —0100 to +0100. During this time the bridge over the gates opens to allow entry 3 times at hourly intervals.

Tides

Streams in the river outside run hard, up to $4^1/_2$ knots at springs, flooding from HW Le Havre —0400 and ebbing from HW +0100. In the approach channel they are 1 knot or less. Times of rise and fall related to HW Le Havre:

MHWS	— 0119	8.1 m
MLWS	— 0500	1.4 m
MHWN	— 0022	6.8 m
MLWN	— 0258	2.9 m

Approach by Day

The entrance from the Seine into the approach channel is now marked by a prominent radar control tower about a quarter of a mile above the point where the Digue du Ratier becomes a seawall. The turn into the approach channel should be made with all the power at your command as there are confused eddies at the junction. The channel is bounded by sloping masonry walls but keep in midchannel as the sides dry 3 - 4 m mud with many obstructions. If these mudbanks are visible you should anchor as the Avant Port will be dry. Landing is possible by dinghy at the steps further up.

After a quarter of a mile, the channel, hitherto dead straight, bifurcates at a lighthouse. Eschew the port channel, which leads to a backwater, and incline to starboard to enter the Avant Port. This is of roughly uniform depth, drying 3 - 4 m in mud so soft that even a deep keel boat will happily sit upright at LW. If you arrive on a rising tide and have to wait for the basin to open, secure to the wall to starboard in front of the gates. Ensure that you are well fendered if you propose to dry out here, as the foot of the wall has buttresses projecting 0.6 m. Indeed it may be safer to secure to one of the many fishing boats provided there is someone on board while the boat is afloat. When the bridge lifts wait for boats to emerge before entering. Secure to the visitors' pontoon ahead, bow to the pontoon and stern to a mooring buoy.

Moorings and Facilities

In the last few years a miniature marina has been built in the heart of Honfleur so that pontoons extend along two sides of the basin, residents on the east and visitors on the south. Water and free electricity are laid to the pontoons, and charges are moderate, about 2 francs per metre per night, the second night as ever being free. You can moor free to the quay on the west side but there you are bereft of water and electricity and must allow for a 1.5 m rise of level while the gates are open. The basin is surrounded on three

Honfleur: The entrance to the approach channel from the Seine.
The new control tower is visible from afar. Digue du Ratier on right.

Honfleur: The lighthouse in the approach channel. The town and the outer
harbour can be seen in the right background.

Honfleur: From the outer harbour showing the bridge to the inner basin

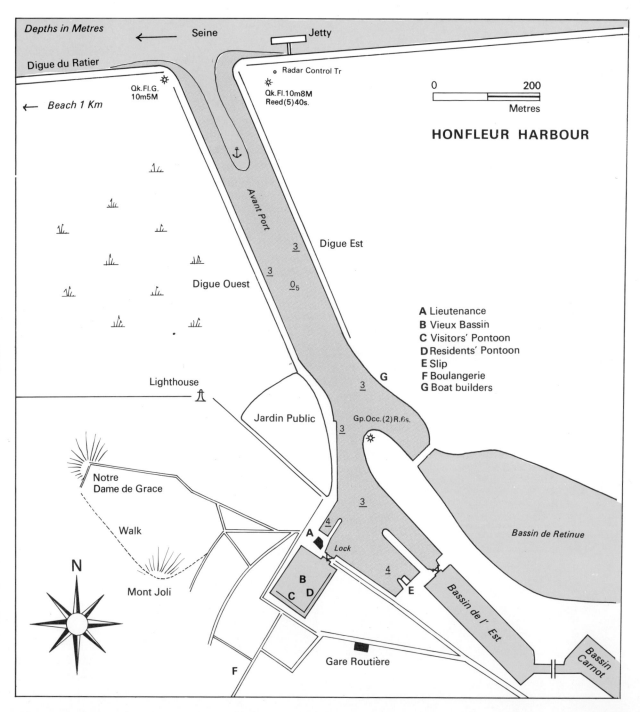

Depths in Metres

← Seine · Jetty

Digue du Ratier

Qk.Fl.G.
10m5M

← Beach 1 Km

Radar Control Tr

Qk.Fl.10m8M
Reed(5)40s.

0   200
Metres

HONFLEUR HARBOUR

Avant Port

Digue Est

Digue Ouest

3

3

0₅

A Lieutenance
B Vieux Bassin
C Visitors' Pontoon
D Residents' Pontoon
E Slip
F Boulangerie
G Boat builders

G

3

Lighthouse

Jardin Public

3

Gp.Occ.(2)R.6s.

Notre
Dame de Grace

Walk

Mont Joli

N

A

Lock

B

C   D

4

E

Bassin de Retinue

Bassin de l' Est

Bassin Carnot

F

Gare Routière

sides by tall narrow buildings of various degrees of antiquity. The Lieutenance, the medieval governors' castle which dominates the harbour, houses the local yacht club (with visitors' lavatories) and the *chef du port*. During your stay in Honfleur you will be subjected by day to constant surveillance and photography by the crowds of tourists strolling on the quay and by night a certain amount of noise from the local chapter of Hell's Angels as they roar round and round the basin till after midnight. If you tire of this, you may moor by negotiation with the *chef du port* in the Bassin de l'Est, a large disused commercial basin accessible by a lock at the far end of the Avant Port. Here you will have absolute peace but no facilities of any kind.

There is a small marine engineers/boat building establishment on the far side of the Avant Port but no cranes or slips.

By Night

Entrance by night is not advised except with local knowledge. The Digue Est at the entrance is lit by Qk Fl and the lighthouse in the channel shows Gp Occ(2) R but there are no other aids.

Honfleur: the inner basin with the *Lieutenance* and the gate

Honfleur: the quieter W quay with the *Lieutenance*

Amenities

Honfleur was once one of the main ports of Normandy. It was from here that the French explorers of the sixteenth and seventeenth century set out to subdue Canada. Many of the streets and alleyways have medieval buildings. The *Lieutenance* roof provides views of the marina and the Avant Port and there is a strange wooden church and two museums. If you tire of sight-seeing and the crowds of tourists, it is possible to walk up behind the town to Mont Joli and Calvaire de Grace for the panoramic view of the estuary and marshland. Alternatively you can walk out along the Digue du Ratier to the beach and watch the turbulent brown river roaring past and wonder whether you ever dare put to sea again. The beach itself is suitable for swimming only at HW, but you can take a pleasant walk towards Deauville, stepping over the occasional nude sunbather as you go, for that which is forbidden in Deauville is tolerated here. The cheapest restaurants are of course in the back streets well away from the marina. There is a good selection, the cheapest of all being the Relais des Routiers at the far end of the Bassin de l'Est.

Canal de Tancarville

The Tancarville canal, built in 1887 to enable ships to pass from Le Havre to the Seine without exposing themselves to the hazards of the Seine Estuary, is now too small for many modern ships and is being replaced by the much larger Canal Central running parallel to it. It still provides for yachts a way to the relatively tranquil reaches of the river which is independent of weather.

The canal is 18 miles (28 Km) long and runs from the Arrière Port at Le Havre via a lock and a maze of dock basins then almost straight across reclaimed marshland to Tancarville, where there are locks down into the river.

Restrictions

1. The lock for small boats, l'Ecluse de la Citadelle, opens on request at all stages of the tide.

2. The Tancarville lock will allow you to pass between HW Le Havre —0430 to +0330 with slight daily variations depending on the range of the tide. The lock keeper at Citadelle will advise.

3. There is a speed limit of 5 knots.

4. There are nine bridges which do not open between 2100 and 0600. Sound three long blasts to coerce these into opening by day. The bridges at the Le Havre end may be kept closed for some time during the rush hours (0700 - 0900, 1200 - 1400, 1700 - 1900).

The passage of the canal may take up to 6 hours and at best is very boring compared with the exhilarating 2 hours from Le Havre to Tancarville by river. It is recommended only as a last resort if sea conditions are rough in the estuary.

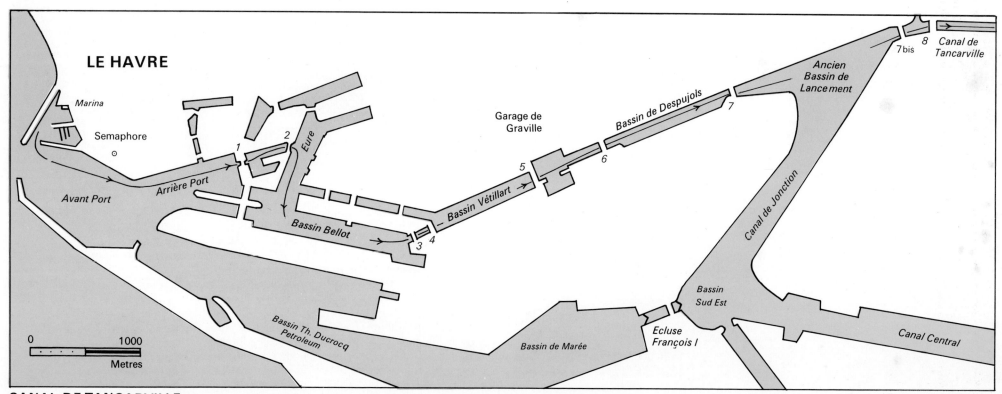

CANAL DE TANCARVILLE

Route

From the marina entrance at Le Havre turn to port into the Avant Port and follow the wall on your port side into the Arrière Port past the Townsend Thoresen terminal when you will see l'Ecluse de la Citadelle (1) ahead. Sound three long blasts and wait for the bridge and gates to open. For the next few kilometres your way is complicated. Pass through the lock Bassin de la Citadelle and keep straight ahead under a bridge (2) into Bassin de l'Eure. Turn to starboard and after 400 m at a 'T' junction turn to port into Bassin Bellot, towards the far end of which you incline to port and pass under two bridges (3) and (4) into Bassin Vétillart. After a further bridge (5) you pass through Garage de Tancarville, which is not actually a garage but a wide basin; then continue straight on through the bridge (6), Bassin M. Despujois, and the bridge (7) to Ancien Bassin de Lancement. Here the main ship channel, the Canal de Jonction, comes in from starboard; so beware of big ships. After the next bridge (7 bis), you will see to port the entrance to the side arm to Harfleur. The canal proper continues under the bridge (8) through picturesque oil refineries and factories until you reach open country, an area of desolate marsh with hills to port. The Tancarville bridge looms large ahead and eventually you reach the Tancarville locks. Keep straight ahead for the small lock; the fork to starboard will take you to the big ship lock. Entry signals: 2 Green lights — entry permitted; 2 Red lights — entry prohibited. Similar lights control passage in the other direction. Lock down into the river and use full power when emerging as there are strong eddies outside the lock and the tide may be making 6 knots.

Harfleur

Harfleur is an ancient town now engulfed by the suburbs of Le Havre. In the Middle Ages it rivalled Honfleur as a port but gradual silting led to the construction of Le Havre in the sixteenth century. The sea has retreated further since due to the building of mudbanks and now it is 6 Km from salt water, although accessible by *péniches* from the Tancarville Canal.

Approach by turning to port between bridges 7 bis and 8 and proceeding up under a high footbridge when you will see ahead barring your way a road bridge with 1 m headroom. Secure to the near end of the concrete quay to starboard in 1.5 m, the far end being shallow. The winding streets of the old town will beguile an hour or so and the fifteenth century church with its ancient clock dominates the quayside. Above the roadbridge the river Lézarde continues past the ancient quays then winds through the old town. There are attractive restaurants here. Harfleur is a convenient overnight stop if you are forced to take the Tancarville canal but find that the tides are wrong for completing the journey in one day.

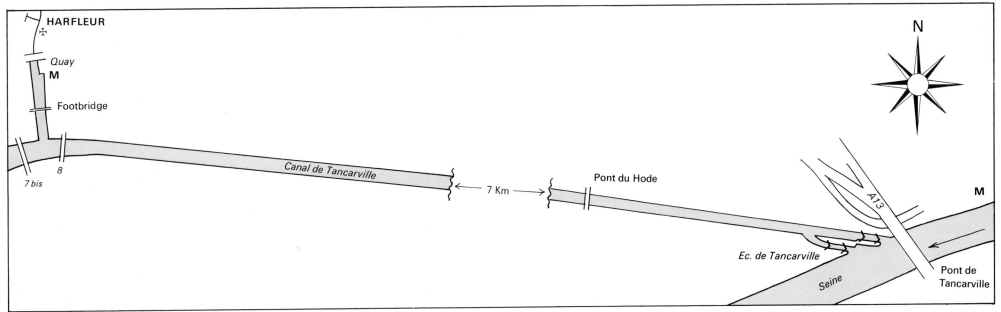

CANAL DE TANCARVILLE

Tancarville to Rouen

Above Tancarville the river leaves the flat country of the estuary reach and becomes more interesting accompanied by hills close at hand on one side or the other for the rest of the way. The tide, which may attain 6 knots at Tancarville, slackens somewhat but still gives a boost, 3 - 4 knots at springs and 2 - 3 knots at neaps.

Caudebec (Km 310) is larger and has restaurants, a pharmacy and even a swimming pool. There is a garage within fuel carrying distance of the river and a small boatyard. It is wiser to moor to some buoys 1 Km below the village as the wharf, although vertical, is only suitable for a short stay at HW because of the depth. About 1 Km above the village is a strange *bas-relief* monument to certain aviators lost in the Arctic in 1928. A new suspension bridge, the only other below Rouen, spans the river here.

At La Mailleraye (Km 303) anchoring is possible near the starboard bank in one of the rare patches of suitable depth, about 2 m charted. There is a tempting restaurant to starboard.

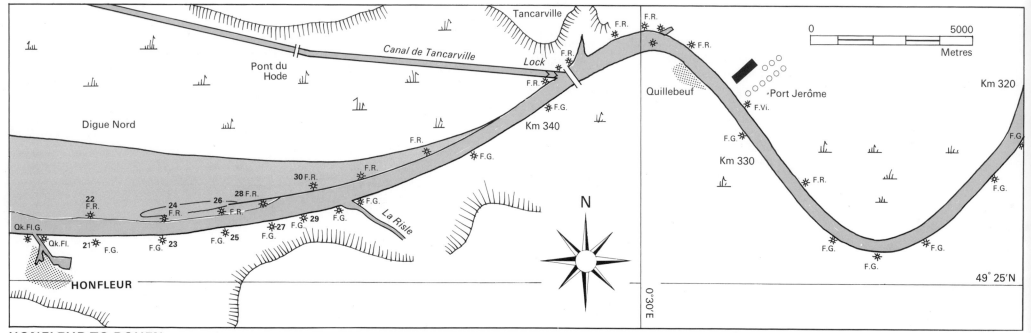

HONFLEUR TO ROUEN

At Km 331 opposite the malodorous oil refinery of Port Jérôme is the attractive village of Quillebeuf with shops and a restaurant. There are some large mooring buoys near the landing steps but the tide runs hard and a dinghy trip ashore might be hazardous.

At Aizier (Km 323), a tiny hamlet overhung by the wooded hills of the Forêt de Brotonne, is a rustic café bar in a garden shaded by trees. Anchoring might be possible here. Villequier (Km 314) is small but has some shops and there are a few mooring buoys to port off the village. Mooring is more comfortable here as each ship slows to drop the pilot who has guided it up from Le Havre and pick up another specialist who will take it up to Rouen. At Villequier in 1843 the daughter of Victor Hugo was drowned by the *mascaret*.

Above Le Trait (Km 298) there are mooring buoys to port fit only for waiting out the flood tide on the trip downriver as there are no other excitements within reach. The river now commences a long bend to port almost doubling back on itself. The Abbaye de Jumièges remains in view above the trees throughout this bend. Along the convex starboard side are many sandy beaches shaded by trees which would be ideal for a picnic but the river is too dirty for swimming and the current almost always too strong.

Duclair (Km 278) is a possible stopping place. A notice on the town quay above the ferry slip may encourage you to secure alongside to step ashore dryshod, stating in terms, 'Mooring is possible here when the tide is above 5 m and below the ferry slip at all times'. But do not be tempted. The foot of the wall dries 5 m and is foul with fallen masonry,

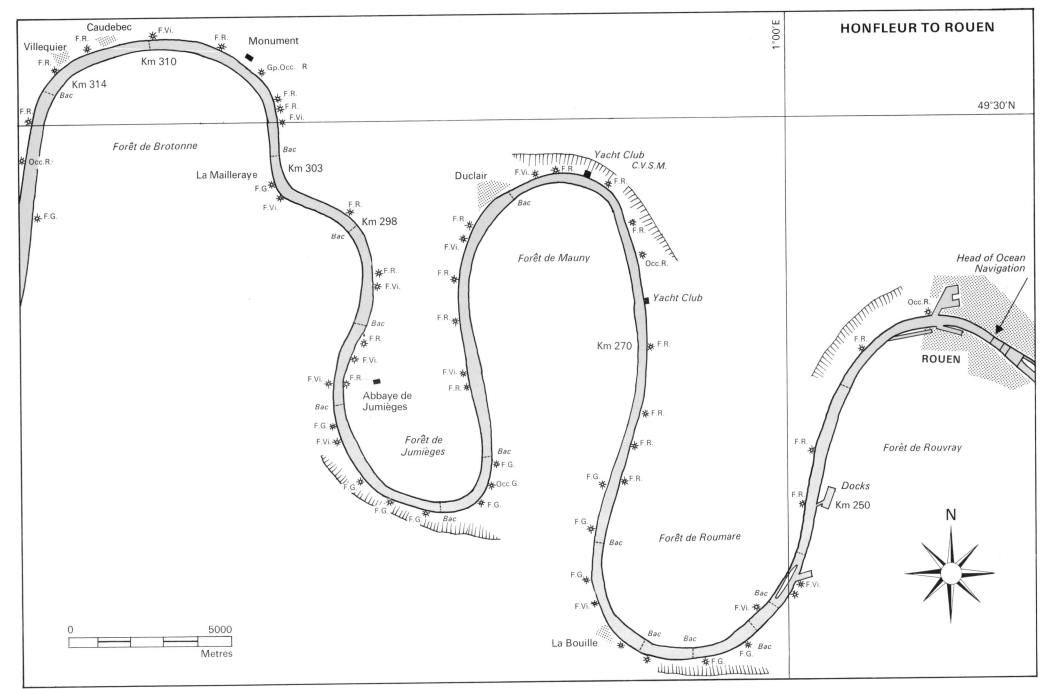

1°00′E

49°30′N

Caudebec
Villequier
F.R.
F.Vi.
F.R.
Monument
Km 310
Gp.Occ. R
Km 314
Bac
F.R.
Occ.R.
F.R.
F.R.
F.Vi.
F.G.
Forêt de Brotonne
Bac
Km 303
La Mailleraye
F.G.
F.R.
F.Vi.
Km 298
Bac
F.R.
F.Vi.
Bac
F.R.
F.Vi.
F.Vi.
F.R.
Bac
F.G.
F.Vi.
Abbaye de
Jumièges
Forêt de
Jumièges
F.G.
F.G.
F.G.
Bac

Duclair
F.Vi.
F.R.
Yacht Club
C.V.S.M.
Bac
F.R.
F.R.
Forêt de Mauny
Occ.R.
F.Vi.
Yacht Club
F.R.
Km 270
F.R.
F.R.
F.R.
F.G.
F.R.
Bac
F.G.
Occ.G.
F.G.
Forêt de Roumare
F.G.
Bac
F.G.
F.Vi.
F.Vi.
Bac
La Bouille
Bac
Bac
F.G.
F.G.

Head of Ocean
Navigation
Occ.R.
ROUEN
F.R.
Forêt de Rouvray
F.R.
Docks
F.R.
Km 250
Bac
F.Vi.

N

0 ————— 5000
Metres

Harfleur: the church and the river Lezarde

while below the ferry there are but piles suitable for a *péniche*. It is wiser to moor to the buoys opposite the town just above the ferry. In the town there is a fine choice of restaurants scattered around the inevitable Place du Géneral de Gaulle. After your meal you can walk along the footpath on the hill above the town to see the views of the river.

At Km 276 to port the yacht club, Cercle de la Voile de la Seine, provides a small crane and a slip. There also appears to be a waterside petrol pump. The club mooring buoys opposite seem to be for small craft of probably less than 4 tons.

At Km 275 beware the Fontaine Sud, a starboard buoy in midstream.

At Km 269 the Château du Corsage Rouge on the hill to starboard recalls the legend of the *Dame* who, when her *Sieur* was away at the Crusades, would make free with her favours, hanging her corset from her window to inform a certain monk of St. Martin de Boscherville across the river that they would not be disturbed. In those days the depressing convention of monastic celibacy was but a convention, and one day when the monk was with his paramour accumulating material for his next confession the *Sieur* returned unexpectedly, killed the monk, dipped the corset in blood and hung it from the battlements as a warning to others.

La Bouille (Km 260) is a picturesque village where the rich of Rouen eat at the open air restaurants under the trees along the river bank. Anchoring may be possible here.

Around the next bend begin the docks of Rouen, where ships from Piraeus, Yokohama and South Shields lie alongside the wharves, which here are backed by a hive of Gallic industry: car factories, refineries and paper mills. Soon the spires of Rouen appear ahead.

Duclair: the town quay. Height of the tide about 4M
The notice invites mooring but the foot of the wall is foul with fallen masonry

Rouen

Rouen is now the fifth port of France and receives 4500 ships annually, its main function being the intercharge of cargoes between ocean going ships and the *péniches*. The city was severely damaged during the war but many older buildings remain and, unlike Le Havre, its rebuilding has been conducted with some taste.

Rouen is almost a compulsory stop on the way upriver for, unless you have dared to stop in the tidal section, you will have been driving for many hours. The next possible place to stop is Elbeuf, a further 22 Km upriver.

Moorings

1. At Km 246 where the river curves from ENE to NE is the entrance to Bassins St Gervais to port. The first of these basins has a few worn pontoons to starboard where you can lie alongside although the nearest to the entrance is reserved for the *douaniers*.

There are no facilities of any kind and it is a 3 Km walk into town but there appears to be no charge. Boats have been broken into here. If your mast has not been lowered this is the only mooring available.

2. If you continue through the city you pass under four bridges of almost identical design. The first of these, le Pont Guillaume le Conquérant (Km 243), is the head of navigation for ocean-going ships and boats with masts. The fourth bridge, Pont Corneille spans an island, Ile Lacroix, and you may moor to a crude iron visitors' pontoon under the port end of the port arch. There is some traffic noise from the bridge overhead but there is no charge and if you like trains you will be encouraged by the occasional freight train trundling by on the quay. Here you are in the heart of the city.

3. On the port side of the island lies the establishment of the Frères Villetard. Here there is fuel, the first above Le Havre, a chandlery and engineers. With small blandishment you may be allowed to moor to a small pontoon just upstream from the fuel pontoon. The tide runs fairly strongly so that springs are needed. A marina is proposed for this spot and in 1978 development had reached the stage at which men with theodolites were at work. The city is at hand just across the bridge yet the mooring is

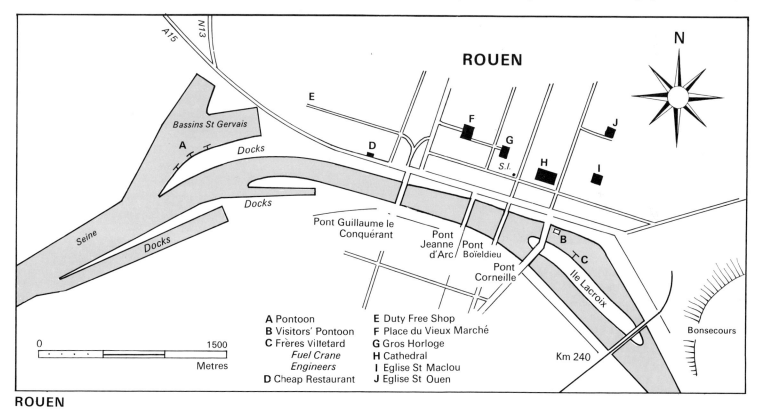

ROUEN

A Pontoon
B Visitors' Pontoon
C Frères Villetard
  Fuel Crane
  Engineers
D Cheap Restaurant
E Duty Free Shop
F Place du Vieux Marché
G Gros Horloge
H Cathedral
I Eglise St Maclou
J Eglise St Ouen

available from Quai de l'Ouest just north of the Bassins St Gervais but only if you state you are going downriver.

Amenities

Much of the medieval part of the city, its narrow cobbled streets and overhanging half-timbered houses, has been preserved. Among the standard tourist attractions are the *cathédrale*, the old market place, the Palais de Justice, the old sixteenth century clock, the Musée des Beaux Arts and L'Eglise St Maclou. The river *quais* are fascinating, as here the *péniches* moor five abreast to wait for a cargo and the *pénichiers* sit and gossip on the wharves. You can take a number 19 bus from just above the visitors' iron pontoon to the hill of Bonsecours where the city and valley will be spread at your feet.

The best restaurants are at the north end of Pont Corneille, although there is a North African quarter just north of St Maclou with more exotic restaurants. The best of all if you are prepared to walk is La Gamellerie on Quai Gaston Boulet just west of Pont Guillaume le Conquérant where for 20 francs, wine included, there is a wide choice of meals. This restaurant is patronised by the more discerning truck drivers and bargees of Rouen.

Rouen: the river above the fourth bridge. The white boat upstream of the *péniche* on the right is moored to the pontoon of Frères Villetard. The offical steel visitors'pontoon is out of sight at your feet.

reasonably quiet. The island, once an industrial area, has a comprehensive range of food shops and a swimming pool.

4. Mooring to the quays seems to be reserved for the *péniches* but you may find a place on the port side opposite Ile Lacroix. Allow for up to 3 m rise and fall. You may be allowed to tie up to a *péniche* but the *pénichiers*, although friendly, will usually find some reason why this is impossible.

Facilities

None of the moorings have water or electricity. The only marine engineers prepared to look at yachts is the Frères Villetard where there is a 5 ton crane. Duty free stores are

Part III **Rouen to Amfreville**

Although now nearly 80 miles from the sea the tyranny of the tides is still considerable for some distance further upriver. At Rouen the tidal range is still as much as 3.3 m at springs but diminishes rapidly to less than 1 m at the head of tide at Amfreville. The level rises for about 4 hours out of 12. At Rouen the flood runs for $4^1/_2$ hours from HW Le Havre +0400 at up to 3 knots at springs, there being little slack water. Between Rouen and Elbeuf the tidal effect spends itself so that above Elbeuf the current almost always runs downriver but rarely exceeds 2 knots in summer. The optimum time of leaving upriver is therefore at the beginning of the flood to carry a fair tide as far as Elbeuf.

Above Rouen you are in the domain of the *péniches*, the 400 ton black steel barges which ply up to Paris and indeed through the thousands of kilometres of inland waterway of France. The hulls are identical: 38 m long, 5 m beam and drawing 4 m fully laden; but the tiny wheelhouse and aftercabin allow the owner, whose floating home this is, to display his individuality. Window boxes and potted plants adorn the cabin windows and the woodwork is brightly painted. Most carry the family car on the roof next to the television aerial and some carry the younger children in a caged playpen on the afterdeck. The whole is driven at a remorseless 7 knots by a gentle thumping of diesel. Sometimes six *péniches*, in all about 2400 tons, are lashed together and pushed from astern by a strange rectangular craft like a floating double decker bus. The *pénichiers* display a Gallic devotion to their task and will usually ignore you except for a friendly wave as you pass but may expect conversation at the locks.

Above Rouen the river continues its meandering course, turning from SE to S then SW before the hairpin bend at Elbeuf which sends it E again. The densely wooded elongated islands which one meets are to be passed on the sides indicated by the arrows at each end. At first there is industry along the banks and for scenery you must lift your eyes to the heights of Bonsecours to port, but later the countryside reappears with its familiar alternation of chalk cliffs and flat fields. You pass under the Autoroute de Normandie twice, taking an hour around the long bend to do the distance that the cars roaring overhead across the bend cover in a minute or so.

At Roches d'Orival (Km 221) the cliffs to port are particularly striking. At St Aubin (Km 220) there is a tempting wall with convenient railings to secure to but this dries out to reveal a rock-strewn bottom.

At Elbeuf (Km 219), the only town of import on this stretch, is a wharf, convenient for the town, where you may safely lie alongside as passing *péniches* cause little wash. Allow for a 2 m range of tide when laying your warps. There is little to interest the professional tourist but there are some good cheap restaurants and pleasant walks along the river. Above Elbeuf the Eure enters, the first tributary of any size since La Risle. After a long straight stretch you will see Amfreville lock ahead and your sojourn on tidal water is over.

Rouen: Bonsecours hill. Ile la Croix to right.

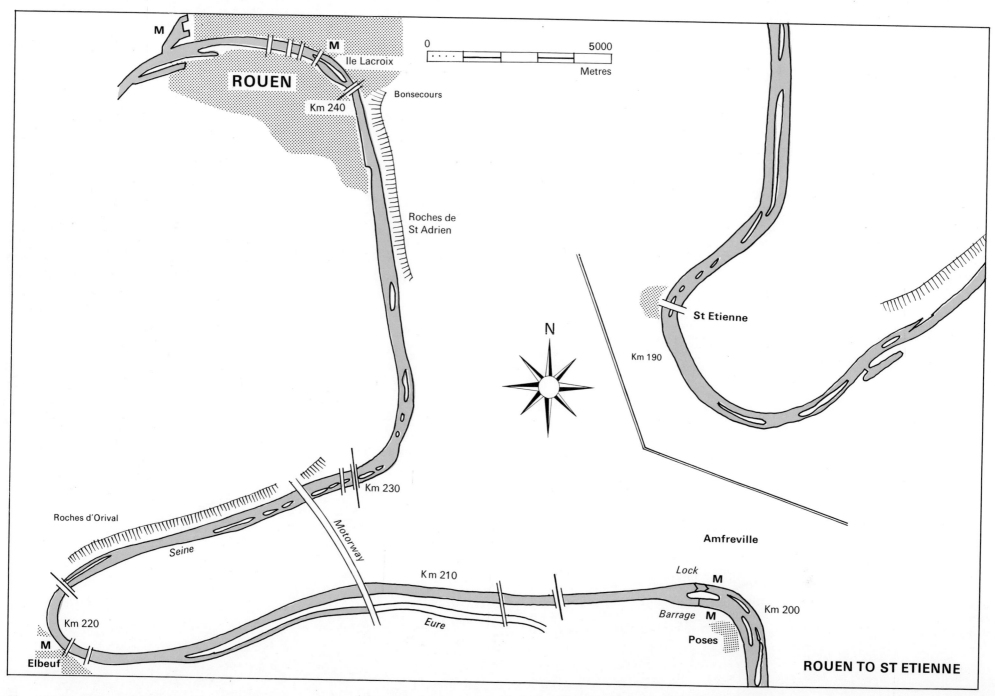

M

ROUEN

M

Ile Lacroix

Km 240

Bonsecours

Roches de
St Adrien

0   5000
Metres

N

St Etienne

Km 190

Km 230

Roches d'Orival

Seine

Motorway

Amfreville

Km 210

Lock   M

Eure

Barrage   M   Km 200

Km 220

Poses

M

Elbeuf

ROUEN TO ST ETIENNE

Part IV Amfreville to L'Oise

Above Amfreville you are at last free from tidal calculations and for the next 202 Km to Paris you have only the adverse current to contend with. In summer about 1 knot (2 Kmph) is usual but in winter you may meet much greater rates. For the first 90 Km the scenery is delightful, and in places spectacular, but above Mantes the outreaching tentacles of Paris make themselves felt. The villages along the river give way to new towns with concrete blocks of flats although still with long rural stretches in between.

Your main problem will be that the river banks are rarely steep-to so that you cannot secure to the bank at will but have to search for a suitable spot. There are many sets of mooring piles but these are reserved for *péniches* and anyway the individual piles are set too far apart for small boats to use safely. You are therefore confined to securing at the small marinas along the river or at the wharves above each lock. As an alternative you can anchor in a backwater but these are not kept dredged and must be approached with extreme caution. Obey the signs which indicate shoaling banks and, if in doubt about the course of the main channel, follow a loaded *péniche*.

Amfreville: a boat rises in the lock.

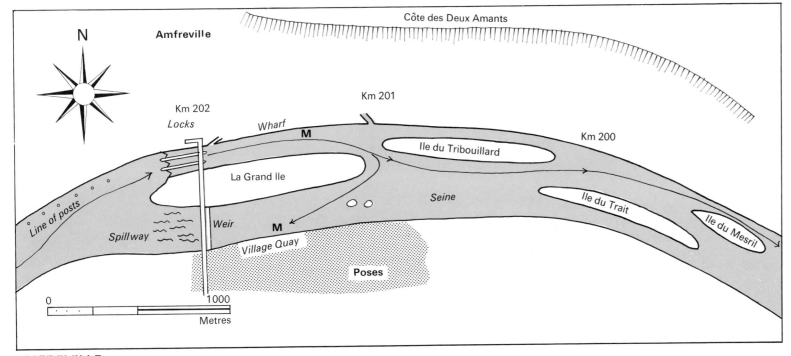

AMFREVILLE

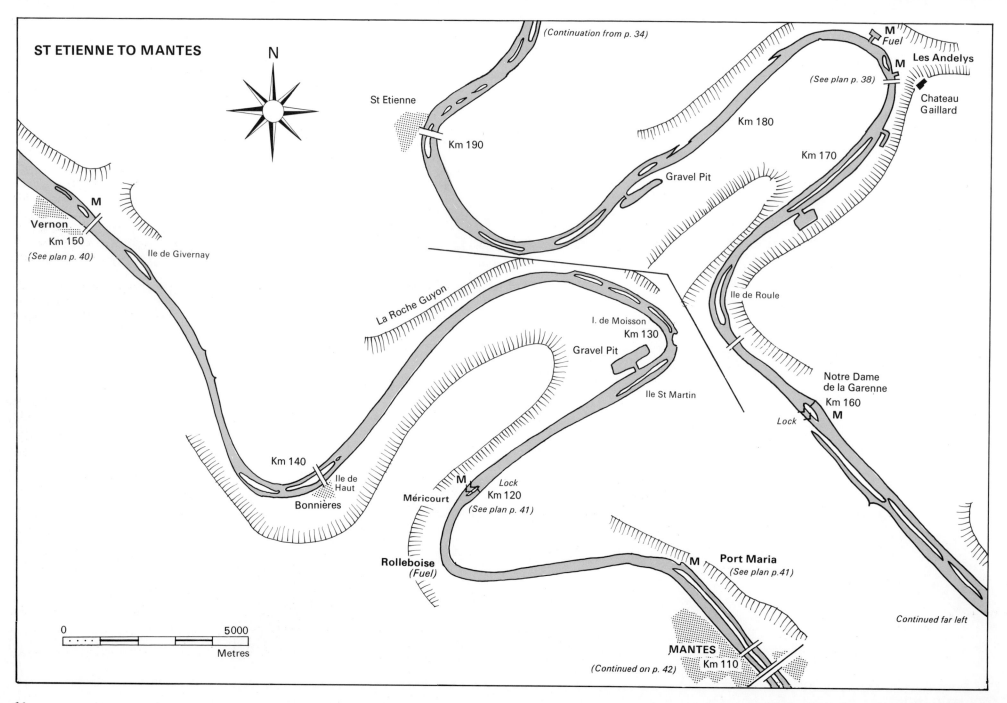

ST ETIENNE TO MANTES

N

(Continuation from p. 34)

St Etienne

M
Fuel

M Les Andelys

(See plan p. 38)

Chateau
Gaillard

Km 190

Km 180

Km 170

Gravel Pit

M
Vernon
Km 150

(See plan p. 40)

Ile de Givernay

La Roche Guyon

Ile de Roule

I. de Moisson
Km 130

Gravel Pit

Ile St Martin

Notre Dame
de la Garenne
Km 160

Lock **M**

Km 140

Ile de
Haut

Bonnières

M
Méricourt

Lock
Km 120

(See plan p. 41)

M Port Maria

(See plan p.41)

Rolleboise
(Fuel)

Continued far left

0   5000

Metres

MANTES

(Continued on p. 42)

Km 110

Amfreville to Les Andelys

Amfreville lock (Km 202) has two locks in parallel, the port being normally used for locking up. The appropriate red and green light signals control entry as in all the other locks on the Seine. It is prudent to cede passage to *péniches* in the vicinity and creep into the lock after them. There are posts to port to secure to while waiting but the turbulent tailrace from the weirs to starboard causes a cross current and adds to your difficulties. The rise in the lock can be 10 m at LW so that very long warps are desirable.

To port above the lock you can secure to a long wharf, a tranquil spot where it is possible to spend a day or two watching the *péniches* go by or by exploring the nearby chalk hills which here resemble the South Downs. The weirs at Amfreville are spectacular, some a slanting fury of white water, others a vertical silky sheet suddenly exploding on the slimy concrete below before bouncing away towards the sea. Yet above the weir the river creeps quietly along as if unaware of the excitement to come. The footbridge across the river gives a vertiginous view of those weirs and leads to the tiny village of Poses which has a bar but no visible shops.

There is an alternative mooring at a wharf in the village attained by turning to starboard at the head of la Grande Ile then passing downriver a short distance.

From Amfreville there is 41 Km of river to the next lock at Notre Dame de la Garenne. This is one of the loveliest stretches, the river winding gently among chalk hills with the occasional riverside hamlet. Navigation requires some care, as there are islands along almost the whole length of this pound and the signs indicating the main channel are by no means obvious. If in doubt wait for a *péniche* and follow it. For some reason the *péniches* often take to travelling on the port side here so beware of meeting head on at bends.

Around a long starboard curve about Km 178 you will see ahead the Château Gaillard, perched on the chalk hills which here flank the port side of the river. This *château* was built in the Middle Ages by Richard Coeur de Lion to control passage of the river. The castle, despite its apparent impregnability on an isolated pinnacle of chalk, never seems to have been able to withstand an organised siege.

Below the castle lie the twin villages of Les Andelys, where there are two marinas, the first since Honfleur. At Km 175 to port a narrow gap in the wooded bank reveals the first marina, a tiny inlet jammed with boats. Entry in a large boat might be difficult and it is wiser to secure temporarily to the jetty 300 m upstream and reconnoitre on foot. Fuel may be available from the pumps here. There is a 2 Km walk to the villages.

Amfreville: péniches rest at the quay above the lock

Les Andelys: Château Gaillard watches the river curve past the chalk cliffs

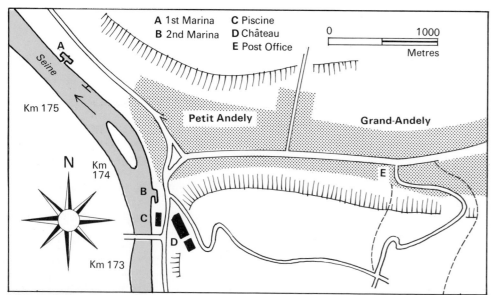

A 1st Marina   **C** Piscine
B 2nd Marina   **D** Château
            E Post Office

0   1000
Metres

Km 175

Km 174

N

Km 173

Petit Andely

Grand-Andely

LES ANDELYS

Les Andelys: Petit Andely village between the river and the chalk plateau.

Les Andelys: the marina in foreground. The white boat is secured to the visitors'pontoon

At Km 174, to port just past an island and before a suspension bridge, is the marina of Les Andelys proper, a larger inlet almost completely occupied by dinghies and small cabin cruisers. The only two berths for boats of seagoing size are at the rickety wooden jetty to port of the entrance in 1.2 m. You will need springs here as the wash of passing *péniches* causes a surge in the shallow water. Plans are in hand to dredge the inlet to make more room for visitors. There are no facilities of any kind but mooring is free as the local sailing club which owns the marina always appears deserted. The river is too dirty to swim in but there is a swimming pool with showers 100 m away for your daily ablutions.

The village of Petit-Andely, spread along the river bank, is linked with Grand-Andely by a main street which runs up a tributary valley. The valley is flanked on each side by chalk downs. Grand-Andely is the local metropolis with a post office and some reasonable restaurants. At Petit-Andely you can eat in the open air under trees overlooking the river for 35 francs.

There are pleasant walks along the river in both directions but if you feel energetic it is worth climbing up the steep track behind the marina to the *château*. Even if you begrudge the 1 franc entry there is a fine view with the river at one's feet and the chalk hills extending into the distance. You can walk for many miles along the ridge to the E with a continuous view across the valley.

Above Les Andelys the river passes close under the rock of Château Gaillard through a narrow gap in the hills and is then deflected on to the SE by the ridge of Bois de la Grande Garenne to enter a long straight reach of 25 Km.

38

La Garenne to Vernon

The next lock, Notre Dame de la Garenne, has a smaller rise than Amfreville and is the beginning of another long pound of 40 Km. To port there is an enormous barrage, whose towers are visible from far downriver, separated by an island from the four parallel locks; the two starboard locks are closed at the moment. One of the locks has a guillotine gate suspended 20 m above the entrance presumably to discipline erring *pénichiers*. You can secure to a quay to port above the lock but no provisions are available within walking distance.

Vernon (Km 150) has one of the most attractive moorings of the whole river. You may secure free of charge to the pontoon of the local sailing club whose headquarters are in a converted *château* opposite the town. The approach merits some care as an island in midstream off the pontoon has recently disappeared, although none of the natives would say whither or how; theft or earthquake are equally likely. The residual shoal is sketchily marked by a line of buoys. From down-stream leave the buoys to starboard and proceed parallel to the shore until you see the pontoon to starboard. Secure above the slip to the pontoon by the stern with a bow anchor out in 3 m. Water and free electricity are laid on and there are showers and lavatories in the outbuildings of the *château*. This is a delightful spot in a quiet backwater of the river overhung by trees with the remains of a twelfth century bridge just upstream. Vernon, across the bridge, is an unexciting town but with good cheap restaurants. There are pleasant walks along the river, as well as a more enterprising hike up the track to the NW through the Fôret de Vernon on its high chalk plateau.

Above Vernon the river makes a horseshoe shaped excursion to the NE to the cliff of La Roche-Guyon with its *château*; it then returns to approach the next lock at Méricourt.

Notre Dame de la Garenne: an empty coal péniche is pushed into the lock

Notre Dame de la Garenne: a pusher with empty coal barges accelerates out of the lock

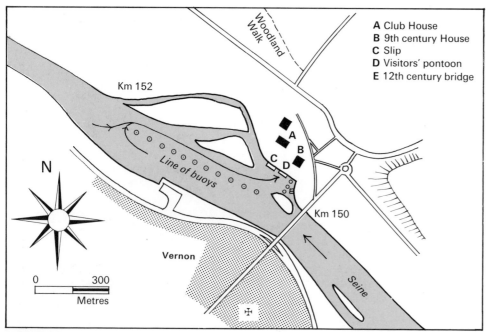

A Club House
B 9th century House
C Slip
D Visitors' pontoon
E 12th century bridge

VERNON

Vernon: the 12th Century bridge and the marina. The visitors' pontoon to right of the moored boats.

Méricourt to Andrésy

The next lock at Méricourt is in layout an almost exact replica of Notre Dame de la Garenne. You may moor to the wall to starboard just above the lock. Provisions are at hand in the village and there also is a Vietnamese restaurant which is of interest to the connoisseur of rice. Rolleboise (not pronounced phonetically) 2 Km upriver has a fuel pontoon but no diesel at the moment.

A little further upstream is Port Maria, a name suggesting a 400 berth marina. In fact there are only two small pontoons with room for perhaps ten boats and the whole outfit is run from the nearby restaurant. To approach, leave to starboard Ile l'Aumone at Km 112 and proceed past the sailing club to port for 300 m to the restaurant prominently labelled Port Maria. Secure to the pontoon angled out from the shore and report to the restaurant. There is a flat rate of 10 francs per night (5 francs extra if you want electricity) but water is free. A 1.5 ton crane is available. The restaurant is exceedingly expensive and

there is a 2 Km walk along the riverbank for food at Mantes. In any case Mantes la Jolie is now misleadingly named as, once a market town, it is now submerged by concrete municipal flats. It was here that in 1087 William the Conqueror had a nasty accident. He had just burnt the town to the ground to exert his will over the inhabitants when his horse trod on a hot cinder and threw him forward on to the pommel of his saddle, causing a painful injury from which he died in Rouen some weeks later. To save his soul he left orders to have the town rebuilt.

Leaving Port Maria you may pass up either side of the long island for 6 Km through Mantes then alongside the Autoroute de Normandie.

At Km 98 leave Ile de Juziers to port and pass under the bridge at Km 93 to reach the marina at Les Mureaux, run by the Cercle de la Voile de Paris, which gives a warm welcome to exotic visitors, providing showers, a bar and, at weekends, even a restaurant in the clubhouse. Moor to pontoons as directed. A 1 ton crane is available.

Les Mureaux, a new town in the making, is not worthy of your attention, but Meulan across the bridge has a pleasant riverside promenade and some reasonable restaurants.

The next moorings are at Médan (Km 83) at a rustic leisure complex called La Plage which provides a swimming pool, waterskiing, canoeing, etc. So highly is it regarded that even the nearby SNCF station is called Médan La Plage. Approach by leaving to port Ile d'Hernières at Km 84 and moor to the pontoons as directed. You may also secure to the jetty of the Moulin Rouge Restaurant provided you eat their 45 franc meal. A notice nearby states *naturisme tolérée avec sexe cachée*, which gains in ambiguity in translation. Villennes village, the nearest source of provisions is 1 Km away and on the way you pass a house in which Emile Zola once lived.

The river now starts to meander again, the wandering to and fro becoming ever more erratic so that Villennes, only 30 Km from Notre Dame by road, is 82 Km by river. After a brief excursion to the S it turns NE past the disused lock at Poissy and begins a great horseshoe bend around the densely wooded Fôret de St Germain, former hunting ground of the kings of France.

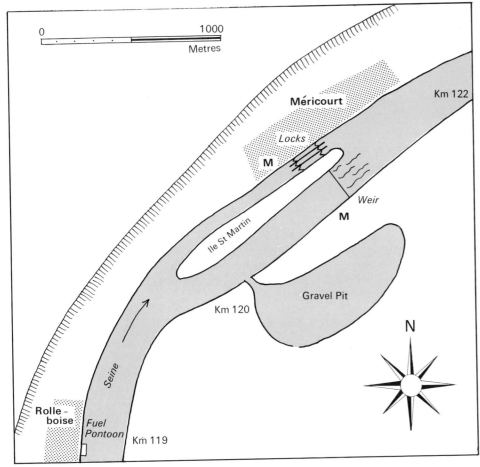

MERICOURT

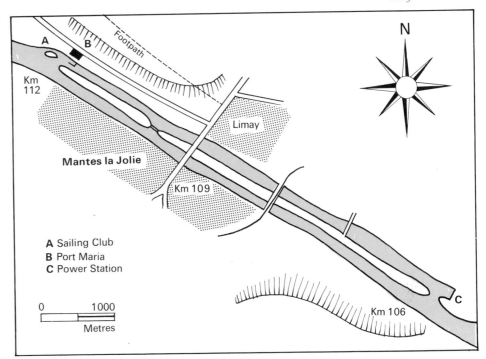

PORT MARIA

Méricourt: a yacht clings to the wall in the wake of a *péniche*

MANTES TO THE OISE

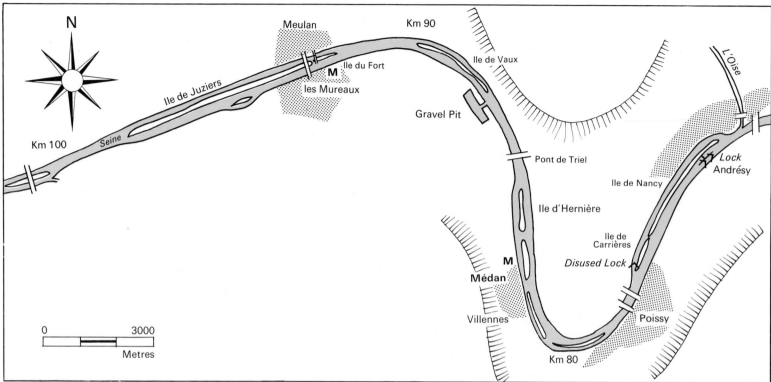

Andrésy: the barrel gate lifts to let a turmoil of water into the lock.

Port Maria.

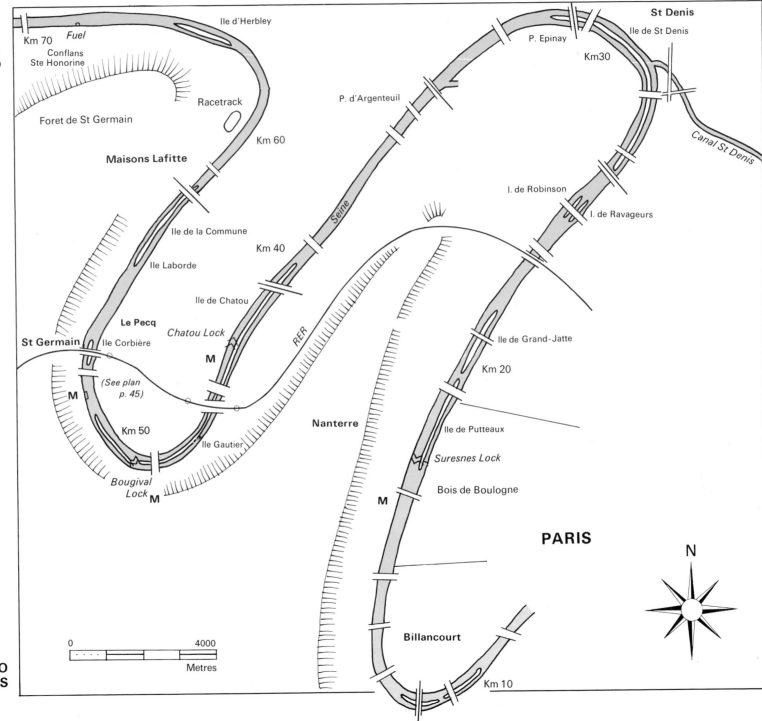

Part V **Paris**
St Germain to Suresnes

St Denis
Ile de St Denis
Km 70
Fuel
Ile d'Herbley
Conflans
Ste Honorine
P. Epinay
Km30
Racetrack
P. d'Argenteuil
Canal St Denis
Foret de St Germain
Km 60
Maisons Lafitte
Seine
I. de Robinson
Ile de la Commune
Km 40
I. de Ravageurs
Ile Laborde
Ile de Chatou
Le Pecq
RER
Ile de Grand-Jatte
St Germain   Ile Corbière
Chatou Lock
Km 20
M
(See plan p. 45)
M
Ile de Putteaux
Nanterre
Km 50
Ile Gautier
Suresnes Lock
Bougival Lock
M
Bois de Boulogne
M
PARIS

N

0   4000
Metres

THE OISE TO PARIS

Billancourt
Km 10

43

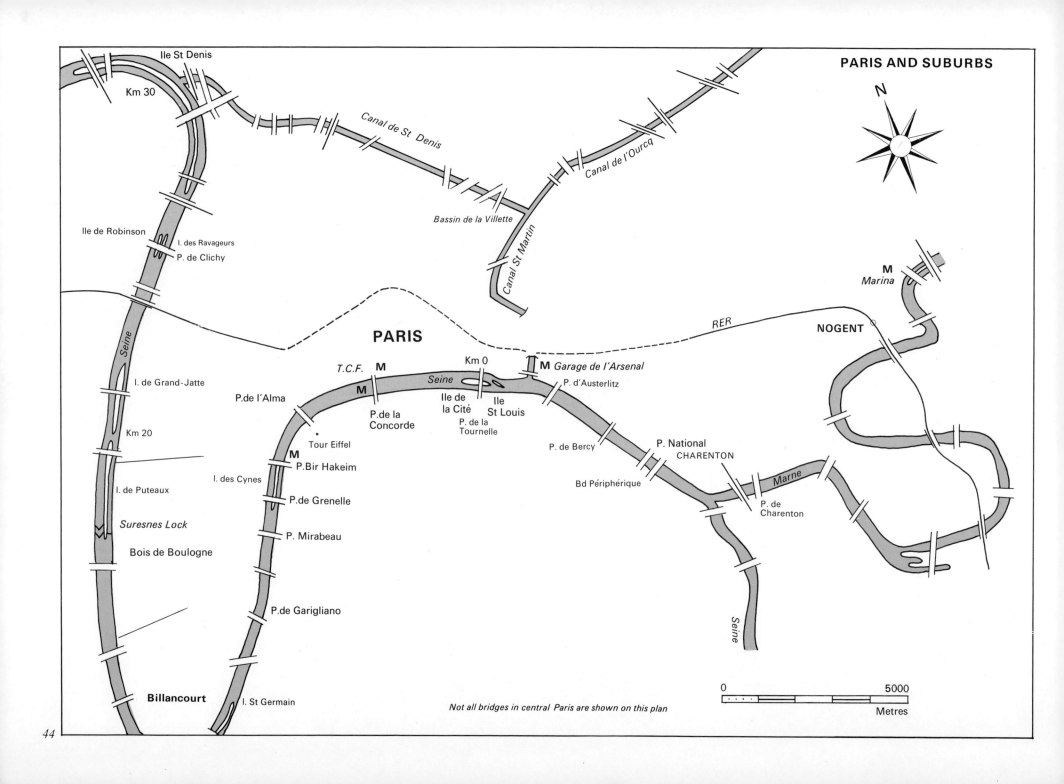

PARIS AND SUBURBS

N

Ile St Denis

Km 30

Canal de St Denis

Canal de l'Ourcq

Bassin de la Villette

Ile de Robinson

I. des Ravageurs

P. de Clichy

Canal St Martin

Seine

M *Marina*

RER

NOGENT

I. de Grand-Jatte

PARIS

T.C.F. **M**

Km 0

M *Garage de l'Arsenal*

P. de l'Alma

Seine

P. d'Austerlitz

M

P. de la Concorde

Ile de la Cité

Ile St Louis

Km 20

Tour Eiffel

P. de la Tournelle

I. de Puteaux

M P. Bir Hakeim

I. des Cynes

P. de Bercy

P. National

CHARENTON

Suresnes Lock

P. de Grenelle

Bd Périphérique

Marne

Bois de Boulogne

P. Mirabeau

P. de Charenton

P. de Garigliano

Seine

Billancourt

I. St Germain

Not all bridges in central Paris are shown on this plan

0   5000

Metres

44

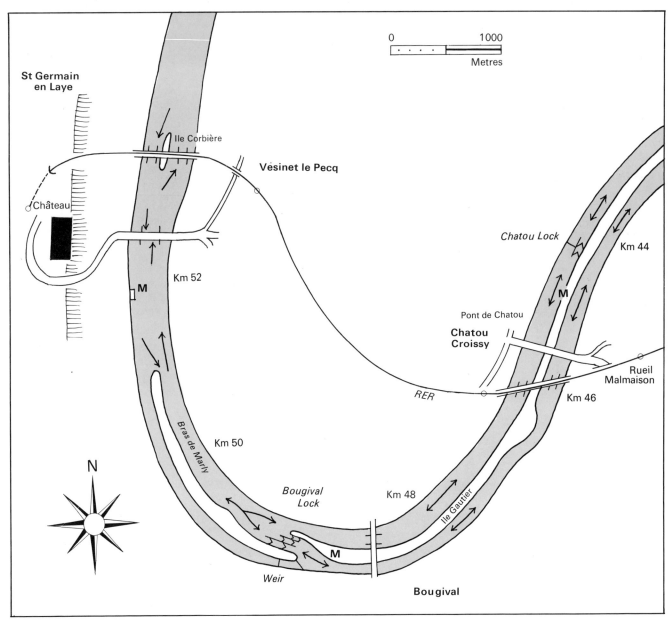

St Germain
en Laye

Ile Corbière

Vésinet le Pecq

Château

Km 52

M

Chatou Lock

Km 44

M

Pont de Chatou

Chatou
Croissy

Rueil
Malmaison

RER

Km 46

Bras de Marly

Km 50

*Bougival
Lock*

Km 48

Ile Gautier

M

Weir

Bougival

N

0   1000

Metres

ST GERMAIN - BOUGIVAL - CHATOU

From Bougival (Km 49) at the apex of the next bend to Km 40 the river is bisected by Ile du Chiard and you have a choice of routes and indeed of locks. Bougival lock links the foot of the island to the starboard bank, whereas Chatou (Km 44) joins the middle of the island to the port bank. There are advantages in either route.

If you pass through Bougival lock, which has three chambers arranged *en échelon*, you can moor to the quay to port above the lock. The surroundings are semirural with dense woods overhanging the river but there is a busy road on the far bank. Across the footbridge the village of Bougival provides food and a wide range of restaurants but there are no other excitements at hand.

If you leave the lock and island to starboard you will shortly reach Chatou lock, a simple affair with a barrage to port and single lock chamber to starboard. You can moor to a narrow quay to starboard below the lock. This spot, although not particularly attractive from the scenic point of view, is convenient for the suburban shopping centre of Chatou just across the bridge and the RER (Reseaux Express Régionaux) station of Chatou, a mere twenty minutes from Paris.

From here upstream the river passes through suburbs of decreasing affluence and increasing dreariness interspersed with samples of the might of French industry until, near St Denis, round a curve there is a first glimpse of the Tour Eiffel above the factories in the foreground. From Km 33 to 25 the river is divided by the Ile St Denis. At Km 29 the Canal de St Denis opens to port. This canal was built in the nineteenth century to enable *péniches* to bypass the long bend of the river through Sèvres. Now little used, it meanders through the northern suburbs of Paris past disused warehouses and under short tunnels to a T junction with the almost unknown Canal de l'Ourcq, which runs for 100 Km through the country north east of Paris, and the Canal St Martin, which rejoins the Seine near the Gare de Lyon.

Suresnes lock (Km 17) has three locks to starboard and a barrage to port; it is sandwiched between the Bois de Boulogne and the suburb of Nanterre, seat of the infamous university. A busy road runs on the starboard side of the river and although you can moor to starboard below the lock it is better to continue towards Paris.

Mooring might be possible at the pontoons of the Club Hélice de France to starboard at St. Cloud 16 Km.

Suresnes is the last lock before Paris and the river now passes Longchamps race track and around the Billancourt curve through a depressing litter of car factories with only the Tour Eiffel on the skyline to remind you that Paris is at hand. Soon one reaches the city boundary and the start of the *pièce de résistance* of the journey, the river trip through Paris.

Paris

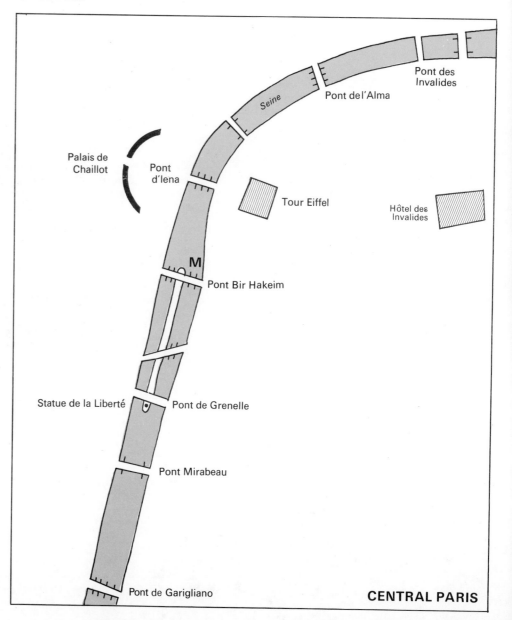

CENTRAL PARIS

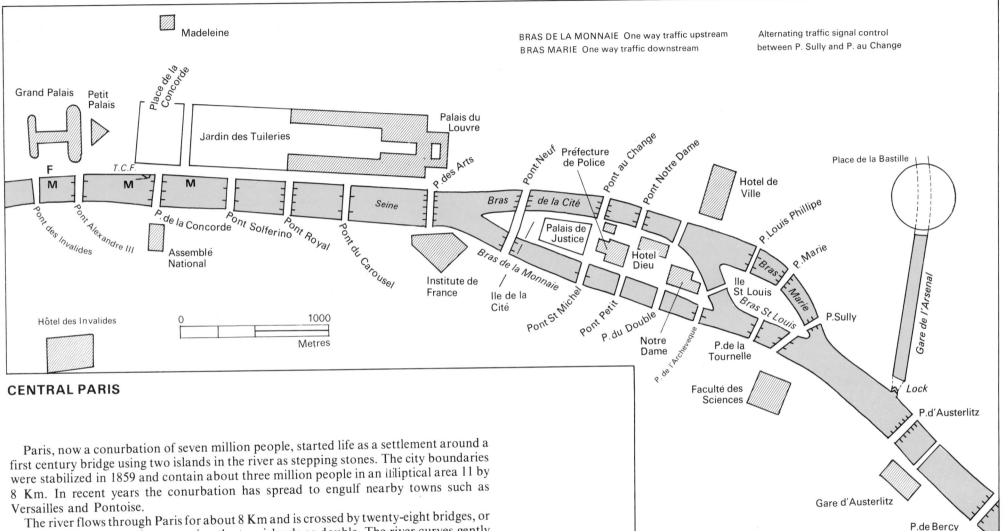

BRAS DE LA MONNAIE One way traffic upstream
BRAS MARIE One way traffic downstream

Alternating traffic signal control
between P. Sully and P. au Change

Madeleine

Grand Palais   Petit Palais

Place de la Concorde

Jardin des Tuileries

Palais du Louvre

F   T.C.F.

M   M   M

Pont des Invalides
Pont Alexandre III
P. de la Concorde   Assemblé National
Pont Solferino
Pont Royal
Pont du Carousel

Seine

P. des Arts

Institute de France

Ile de la Cité

Bras de la Monnaie

Pont St Michel

Pont Neuf

Bras   de la Cité

Préfecture de Police

Pont au Change

Pont Notre Dame

Palais de Justice

Hotel Dieu

Pont Petit

P. du Double

P. de l'Archeveque

Notre Dame

Faculté des Sciences

P. de la Tournelle

Ile St Louis

Bras   P. Marie

Bras St Louis

Marie

P. Louis Phillipe

Hotel de Ville

Place de la Bastille

P. Sully

Gare de l'Arsenal

Lock

P. d'Austerlitz

Gare d'Austerlitz

P. de Bercy

Hôtel des Invalides

0   1000

Metres

CENTRAL PARIS

Paris, now a conurbation of seven million people, started life as a settlement around a first century bridge using two islands in the river as stepping stones. The city boundaries were stabilized in 1859 and contain about three million people in an lilliptical area 11 by 8 Km. In recent years the conurbation has spread to engulf nearby towns such as Versailles and Pontoise.

The river flows through Paris for about 8 Km and is crossed by twenty-eight bridges, or thirty-six if you count those crossing the two islands as double. The river curves gently but continuously to starboard so that new perspectives come into view under each bridge. The famous *quais* for the use of strollers, fishermen or those who just sit in the sun run the length of the river banks. A colony of 'tarted up' *péniches* used as houseboats has grown up along the *quais* and a battle is currently being waged by the mayor of Paris to remove them on the grounds that they clutter the riverside scene: a matter of opinion. It follows that casual mooring along the *quais*, however tempting, is likely to be frowned on by the city council.

To even summarize the tourist attractions of Paris would require a book in itself, so that this chapter describes Paris from a visiting sailorman's viewpont. However, many of the famous buildings can be seen from the river.

The Tour Eiffel dominates the sky to starboard as you approach the Allée des Cygnes, an elongated island bisecting the river for the space of three bridges. Beyond the last of these, the Pont Bir Hakeim, is a colony of unofficially moored *péniches* whose occupants might let you secure outside them.

Opposite the Tour Eiffel is the vast arc of the Palais de Chaillot and directly ahead on the skyline you will glimpse on a clear day the white dome of Sacré Coeur. The next landmarks are the great dome of Les Invalides, where Napoleon lies buried, to starboard and the Grand Palais and Petit Palais directly opposite to port.

Paris: TCF visitors' pontoon. A Bateau Mouche heads towards Pont Alexandre III

Paris: the Touring Club de France office and visitors' pontoon. Pont Alexandre III in background

To port at this point, between Pont des Invalides and Pont Alexandre III, are some of the moorings under the fiefdom of the Touring Club de Paris and a fuel pontoon. Before the next bridge, Pont de la Concorde, are the headquarters of the Touring Club de France, who also own the moorings to port up to the Passerelle de Solferino.

Beyond here the Palais Royal and the Louvre run alongside the port bank for 1 Km and soon you see ahead the first of the two islands, Ile de Cité. For the best view of Notre Dame leave the Ile to port and pass below the walls of the Palais de Justice until the breathtaking view of the west face of the *cathédrale* bursts upon you. Notre Dame is at Km 0 on the river and is the point from which all distances from Paris are measured.

The lesser known Ile de St Louis now appears to port and soon you come to the orifice of the Canal St Martin guarded by a lock. This really marks the end of tourist Paris as docks and warehouses line the banks hereafter although the spaghetti junctions of the Boulevard Périphérique just upstream may interest the connoisseur of confusion.

Moorings

You may officially moor in Paris only at the Touring Club de France which controls the moorings on the port side between Pont des Invalides and Passerelle de Solferino. Report first at their jetty below Pont de la Concorde. Facilities here are reasonable with water and electricity as are the charges (1 franc per m per day). There are however disadvantages. The noise of the traffic from the Place de la Concorde above continues night and day; one of the unofficial tourist sights of Paris is Place de la Concorde in the evening rush hour as the Renaults and Simcas and Citroëns gallop eight abreast over the evening rush hour as the Renaults and Simcas and Citroëns gallop eight abreast over the cobbles in swirling streams of roaring metal. Furthermore the *bateaux mouches*, sightseeing boats like floating greenhouses but the size of minesweepers, trundle past every few minutes keeping a constant wash sloshing to and fro from bank to bank. If you decide to moor here, remember your earplugs and ensure that you are well secured and fendered with tyres. An ordinary fender will hardly last a day against the coarse stone

Paris: Péniches in double harness leave Pont de la Concorde astern. TCF office and visitors'pontoon are seen at the left end of the bridge.

quais of Paris. A high price to pay, you might think, for being in the heart of things.

Alternatives, which might be quieter and of course cheaper are:

1. Friendly houseboatmen above the Pont Bir Hakeim.
2. A colony of more disreputable boats to starboard below the Pont Neuf. These are under the threat of expulsion by the Mayor but there might be safety in numbers for a few nights.
3. The first basin, Gare de l'Arsenal of Canal St Martin. The canal is little used and you must ask in advance at the headquarters of the *Port Autonome* of Paris at Pont Bir Hakeim whether the lock into the basin will be opened. The Canal passes north through the less savoury eastern suburbs of Paris to its junction with Canal de l'Ourcq then becomes the Canal de St Denis which rejoins the Seine at St Denis.

Amenities

The land based attractions of Paris cannot be described here but a few guidelines may be useful. The best way of getting about, except of course by merely strolling, is by *Métro*, the underground railway dating from Edwardian times. The network is more dense than in London, so that no spot within the city limits is more than 500 m from a station. Trains are very frequent and the platforms are usually only one flight of stairs below the street so it is always worthwhile hopping on to a train. Fares are 2 francs single flat rate but if you buy a carnet of ten you save money. The system has been modernized in recent years. A new garishly painted network, the RER, connects with the Metro and serves certain outer suburbs, enabling you to moor out at Vésinet or Nogent and still reach central Paris in twenty minutes for 5 francs. Buses are infrequent probably because the Metro is so convenient.

It is still possible to eat cheaply in Paris; in the side streets just south-west of the Ile de la Cité there are a few 20 franc restaurants. Although the food is good, the service is brisk and the clientèle is mainly English or American.

Nogent sur Marne

, An alternative mooring in the eastern suburbs can be found at Nogent sur Marne, the only disadvantage being the additional journey up the river of 27 Km. However, so tortuous is the river that Nogent is only 8 Km by rail from central Paris.

4 Km beyond the entrance to Canal St Martin one reaches the confluence of the Marne. From here the Seine continues another 400 Km to its source near Dijon, but is navigable only as far as Marcilly, 170 Km upstream. If you are heading for the Mediterranean, turn right at Montereau, 104 Km away, and keep going for another 800 Km, 233 locks and at least three weeks. France is a very large country! Above Marcilly the river gradually dwindles towards its source, which is not, as some think, a tap in a field, but a ruined Roman temple to the *sequana*.

At the confluence turn to port into the Marne, a smaller river than the Seine but just as busy, pursuing an apparently aimless course through the eastern overspill of Paris. After 20 Km of river, little ground has been gained and you are still in suburbia on reaching Nogent.

Here the Centre Sportif et Touristique du Val de Marne owns a sports complex with swimming pool, bowling alley, restaurant and a small marina. This last is given over almost entirely to small motorboats which jam the space between an island and the bank.

Nogent: hauling out. The octagonal *Capitainerie*

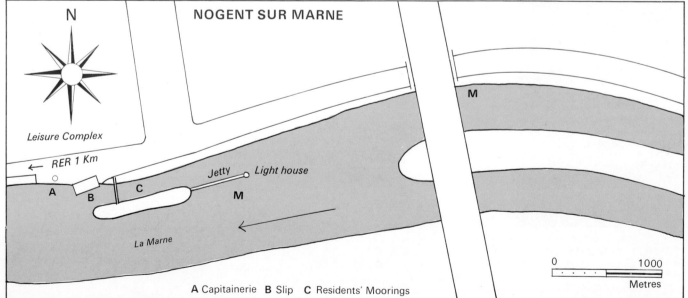

NOGENT SUR MARNE

Leisure Complex

← RER 1 Km

Jetty ○ Light house

A B C M

La Marne

A Capitainerie B Slip C Residents' Moorings

0 — 1000 Metres

However you can secure to the outside face of the jetty running upstream from the island, the bank of the island itself being shoal. For about 1 franc per m per night you get water, free electricity and the use of the lavatory (when the *chef du port* is present to lend you the key). There seems no reason why you cannot secure for free to the long quay to port above the jetty.

The marina is situated in a reasonably pleasant spot, with many trees overhanging the water but is slightly away from things. You can however obtain provisions by strolling 500 m through the park downstream. The nearest station, 1 Km away, is Nogent from which the RER will whisk you to central Paris in ten minutes.

Above Nogent, the Marne continues for 178 Km through the hills of Champagne to Epernay to join the Canal Latéral à la Marne from which routes diverge to the Rhine and the Saône.

Nogent: Visitors secure to the far side of the lighthouse jetty or the left bank under the bridge

Glossary

If you have no French, you will probably find it easier to write down the name of any object you wish to buy or find, as French, with its nasal consonants and generally aphonetic spelling, is one of the most difficult of European languages to pronounce. The French view with reserve attempts to mangle their fair tongue. If you speak French, this glossary may help you with the specialized vocabulary of the sea and boats. Attempts to translate literally into French often fail, as the man who referred to a monkey wrench as *une clef de singe* discovered.

French-English

l'accostage, *mooring (to a quay)*.
accoster, *to come alongside*.
l'acide, *acid*.
l'acier, *steel*.
l'alcool à brûler, *methylated spirit*.
amarrer, *to moor*.
amont, *upstream*.
l'ancre, *anchor*.
l'anneau, *mooring ring*.
appareiller, *to get under way*.
l'arbre d'hélice, *propeller shaft*.
l'arrière, *stern*.
arrière, *aft, astern*.
l'assurance, *insurance*.
l'aussière, *warp*.
aval, *downstream*.
avant, *forward*.
l'avant, *bow*.
l'aviron, *oar*.

bâbord, *port*.
le bac, *ferry*.
la balise, *beacon*.
le banc de sable, *sand bank*.
le barrage, *weir*.
le bassin flot, *wet basin*.
la basse mer, marée basse, *low tide*.
le bateau-feu, *light vessel*.
le berceau, *cradle*.
les béquilles, *legs*.
le bief, *pound*.
la bitte d'amarrage, *bollard*.
la bouée, *buoy*.
la bougie, *sparking plug*.
le busc, *sill of lock*.
la boussole, *compass*.
le brise-*lames*., *break-water*.
le brouillard, *fog*.

les cailloux, *pebbles, shingle*.
le cale, *slipway, wedge*.
calfater, *to caulk*.
le canot, *dinghy*.
le canot de sauvetage, *lifeboat*.
le capitaine de port, *harbour-master*.
la carte marine, *chart*.
le chaumard, *fairlead*.
le chantier, *timberyard, dockyard*.
le chemin de halage, *towpath*.
les chevaux, *horsepower*.
la clef, *spanner*.
la clef à molette, *adjustable spanner*.
le cloison, *bulkhead*.
le contre-plaqué, *plywood*.
la coque, *hull*.
le cordage, *rope*.
les corps-mort, *moorings*.
la côte, *coast*.
le côté, *side*.
le coude, *bend*.
le coup de vent, *gale*.
le cuivre, *copper*.

la dame de nage, *rowlock*.
la darse, *wet dock*.
débarquer, *to disembark*.
la défense, *fender*.
démarrer, *to unmoor*.
le démarreur, *starter*.
dépasser, *to overtake*.
la digue, *bank, dyke*.
la douane, *customs*.
le douanier, *customs officer*.
la drisse, *halyard*.
le drapeau, *flag*.

l'eau douce, *fresh water*.
l'échelle, *ladder*.
l'échelle de marée, *tide gauge*.

l'écluse, *lock*.
embarquer, *embark*.
en bas, *below*.
l'épi, *training wall*.
l'épicerie, *grocer's*.
l'épissure, *splice*.
l'équipage, *crew*.
l'escalier, *steps*.
l'essence, *petrol*.
l'étai, *stay*.
l'étale, *slack water*.
l'évitage, *swinging room*.

la falaise, *cliff*.
faire eau, *to leak*.
le fer, *iron*.
le feu, *light*.
le feu de mouillage, *riding light*.
le feu de navigation, *side light*.
le fil, *wire*.
le flot, *flood tide*.
le foc, *jib*.
franchir, *to clear*.
frapper une amarre, *to belay*.
faire le plein, *to fill up*.
le fanal, *masthead light*.
la fuite d'eau, *leak*.

la gaffe, *boathook*.
le gasoil, *diesel fuel*.
le gouvernail, *rudder, helm*.
gouverner sur, *to steer for*.
la goupille fendue, *split pin*.
la grande voile, *mainsail*.
le gril de carenage, *grid*.
la grue, *crane*.

les haubans, *shrouds*.
les hauts fonds, *shoals*.
haute mer, *high tide*.

l'hélice, *propeller*.
hisser, *to hoist*.
l'homme-grenouille, *frogman*.

l'interrupteur, *switch*.

le jusant, *ebb tide*.

laisser par bâbord, *leave to port*.
le largeur, *beam*.
le longueur, *length*.
le lest, *ballast*.

le maillon, *shackle*.
la manche, *hosepipe*.
le manchon, *bush, collar*.
la manille, *shackle*.
la marée morte, morte eau, *neap tide*
se méfier de, *avoid*.
mettre en panne, *to heave to*.
mettre à l'eau, *to launch*.
mouiller l'ancre, *to anchor*.
le marteau, *hammer*
la mèche, *drill*.

nettoyer, *to scrub*.
le niveau, *level*.
le noeud, *knot*.
le noeud de chaise, *bowline*.

l'orangeau, *mooring ring*.

le palan, *tackle*.
le papillon, *wing nut*.
la passerelle, *gangway*.
la passoire, *filter*.
le pertuis, *sluice*.
le pétrole, *paraffin*.
le phare, *lighthouse*.
le plat bord, *gunwhale*.
la pleine mer, *high tide*.
le plomb, *lead*.
le plongeur, *diver*.
la poulie, *block*.
la prévision du temps, *weather forecast*.
la prise d'eau, *water point*.
le profondeur, *depth*.

la quille, *keel*.

ranger, *to pass close to*.
le recharge, *refill*.

remettre à neuf, *refit*.
remorquer, *to tow*.
la rive, *bank*.

sécher, *to dry out, go aground*.
le sondage, *sounding*.
souffler, *to blow*.
souder, *to weld*.
le soupage, *valve*.

la tenue, *holding ground*.
à terre, *aground*.
le tirant d'eau, *draft*.
le tirant d'air, *headroom*.
le trematage, *overtaking*.
tribord, *starboard*.
la tournevisse, *screwdriver*.
le tuyau, *pipe*.

la vase, *mud*.
la vive eau, *spring tide*.
virer, *to turn*.
le vis, *screw*.
la voie d'eau, *leak*.
le voilier, *sailing boat, sailmaker*.

zingué, *galvanized*.

English-French

acid, *l'acide*.
adjustable spanner, *la clef à molette*.
aft, *arrière*.
aground, *à terre*.
anchor, *l'ancre*.
anchor (to), *mouiller l'ancre*.

ballast, *le lest*.
bank, *la rive, la digue*.
beacon, *la balise*.
bulkhead, *le cloison*.
bearing, *le relèvement*.
belay (to), *frapper une amarre*.
below, *en bas*.
bend, *le coude*.
beware of, *se méfier de*.
block, *la poulie*.
blow (to), *souffler*.
boathook, *la gaffe*.
bollard, *la bitte d'amarrage*.
bolt, *le boulon*.
bow, *l'avant*.
bowline, *le noeud de chaise*.

breakwater, *le brise-lames*.
beam, *le largeur*.
buoy, *la bouée*.
bush, *le manchon*.

carburettor needle, *le pointeau*.
cast off, *lâcher*.
caulk (to), *calfater*.
chart, *la carte marine*.
clear an obstacle, *franchir*.
cliff, *la falaise*.
coast, *la côte*.
copper, *le cuivre*.
cradle, *le berceau*.
crane, *la grue*.
crew, *l'équipage*
customs, *la douane*.
customs officer, *le douanier*.

depth, *le profondeur*.
diesel fuel, *le gasoil*.
dinghy, *le canot*.
disembark, *débarquer*.
diver, *le plongeur*.
dockyard, *le chantier*.
downstream, *aval*.
draft, *le tirant d'eau*.
drill, *la mèche*.
dry out, *sécher*.
dyke, *la digue*.

ebb tide, *le jusant*.
embark, *embarquer*.

fairlead, *le chaumard*.
fender, *le défense*.
ferry, *le bac*.
fill up, *faire le plein*.
filter, *la passoire*.
flag, *le drapeau*.
flood tide, *le flot*.
fog, *le brouillard*.
fresh water, *l'eau douce*.
frogman, *l'homme-grenouille*.

gale, *le coup de vent*.
gangway, *la passerelle*.
get under way, *appareiller*.
go aground, *sécher*.
grid, *le gril de carenage*.
grocer's, *l'épicerie*.
gunwhale, *le plat bord*.

halyard, *la drisse*.

hammer, *le marteau.*
harbourmaster, *le capitaine de port,*
harbourmaster's office, *la capitainerie.*
headroom, *le tirant d'air.*
heave to, *mettre en panne.*
hoist (to), *hisser.*
holding ground, *la tenue.*
horsepower, *les chevaux.*
hosepipe, *la manche.*
hull, *la coque.*

insurance, *l'assurance.*
iron, *le fer.*

jib, *le foc.*

keel, *la quille..*
knot, *le noeud.*

ladder, *l'échelle.*
launch (to), *mettre à l'eau.*
lead, *le plomb.*
leak, *la fuite d'eau, la voie d'eau.*
leak (to), *faire d'eau.*
leave to port (to), *laisser par bâbord.*
legs, *les béquilles.*
lifeboat, *le canot de sauvetage.*
lighthouse, *le phare, le feu.*
lightvessel, *le bateau-feu.*
lock, *l'écluse.*
low water, *la basse mer.*

mainsail, *la grande voile.*
make fast (to), *amarrer.*
masthead light, *le fanal.*
moor (to), *amarrer.*
moorings, *les corps morts.*
mooring ring, *l'organeau.*

neap tide, *la morte eau.*
nut, *l'écrou.*

oar, *l'aviron.*
overtake, *dépasser.*
oysterbed, *le parc à huitres.*

pass close to, *serrer.*
pebbles, *les cailloux.*
petrol, *l'essence.*
plywood, *le contre plaque.*
port, *bâbord.*
pound, *le bief.*
propeller, *l'hélice.*
pump, *la pompe.*

reefknot, *le noeud de plat.*
refit, *remettre à neuf.*
river bank, *la rive.*
rope, *le cordage.*
rowlock, *la dame de nage.*
rudder, *le gouvernail.*

sandbank, *le banc de sable.*
screw, *le vis.*
screw (to), *visser.*
screwdriver, *le tournevis.*
scrub, *nettoyer.*
shackle, *le maillon.*
shingle, *les cailloux.*
shoal, *les hauts fonds.*
shrouds, *les haubans.*
side, *le côté.*
side light, *le feu de navigation.*
sill, *le radier.*
slack water, *l'étale.*
slipway, *la cale.*
sluice, *le pertuis.*
spanner, *la clef.*
sparking plug, *le bougie.*
splice, *l'épissure.*
starboard, *tribord.*
starter, *le démarreur.*
stay, *l'étui.*
steer for, *gouverner sur.*
steel, *l'acier.*
steps, *l'escalier.*
stuffing box, *la presse-étoupe.*
swell, *la houle.*
swinging room, *l'évitage.*
split pin, *la goupille fendue.*
stake, *le poteau.*
switch, *l'interrupteur.*

tackle, *le palan.*
tap, *le robinet.*
tow (to), *remorquer.*
tidegauge, *l'échelle de marée.*
timberyard, *le chantier.*
towpath, *le chemin de halage.*
training wall, *la digue, l'épi.*

unmoor, *largeur, lâcher.*
unscrew, *dévisser.*
upstream, *amont.*

warp, *l'aussière.*
washer, *la rondelle.*
water hydrant, *la prise d'eau.*
weather forecast, *le prévision du temps*

wedge, *la cale.*
weir, *le barrage.*
weld (to), *souder.*
wet basin, *le bassin à flot.*
wingnut, *le papillon.*
wire, *le fil.*